On the Road to Mandalay

On the Road to Mandalay

by

Randle Manwaring

Pen & Sword
MILITARY

First published in Great Britain in 2006 by
Pen & Sword Military
an imprint of
Pen & Sword Books Ltd
47 Church Street
Barnsley
South Yorkshire
S70 2AS

Typeset in 12/14pt Sabon by
Lamorna Publishing Services

Printed and bound in England by CPI UK.

For a cc   ıse contact
47 Chu   S70 2AS,
                                                  uk

Contents

List of poems

Preface

When my memoirs were published in 1990 under the title of *The Good Fight* (the publisher's choice of words, not mine!) I hoped I had sketched out all my relevant experiences to date, my own choice of title having been *A Christian's Rewards and Rejections*. In the book I began with The London Library where my father, also a naval historian, was one of the two assistant librarians, and I moved *fast forward* to my career in the RAF Regiment, finally in Burma, following this with my mix of life in the insurance industry, poetry, India, Australia etc.

Looking back I see my earlier book as rather superficial and I have, therefore, attempted whilst majoring on the war in the Far East, to place my six RAF years in the context of my lifetime career, marking some of the enormous social changes encountered and picking out, pre-war and post-war, my major preoccupations. I have to leave my readers to judge whether I have placed the recurrent theme of war, in personal and national terms, in a convincing setting.

R.M.

Chapter 1

War Leading to War

I was born on 3 May 1912, two or three weeks after the world was shaken by the loss, near the coast of Newfoundland, of the luxury White Star liner *Titanic*. At her launch she was showered with eulogies but some thought that overconfidence encouraged the ancient Greek fear of provoking high heaven. She was so huge, they said, that the sea, far from endangering her, would hardly disturb the comfort of those on board and they would scarcely know, unless they wanted to, that they were all at sea. But an iceberg, drifting across her in the night, destroyed her with the loss of 1,635 lives. Lifeboats, instead of being a means of saving lives were thought to be an extra problem for these huge liners. How could they be easily launched from such a height? The *Titanic* was a ship of 46,800 tons but legislation covering lifeboats had previously only considered ships of up to 10,000. Therefore this unsinkable ship carried lifeboats for only half the passengers.

It might be argued that the arrogance of man at the beginning of the twentieth century was typified by the *Titanic* disaster. His way of life was only mildly disturbed by the disappointments of the Boer War and it waited another two years before that prophet of doom, Thomas Hardy, would mutter his sad predictions about the *Breaking of Nations*, which was imminent.

My father, one of the two official Assistant Librarians at the London Library, received a letter on the day of my birth from the Librarian, Sir Charles Hagberg Wright: 'Dear Manwaring', he wrote, 'enclosed is a trifle to mark the happy event.' (I'm not sure what it was.) My father suffered from a congenital heart complaint and was therefore excused military service in the Great War but, being also a naval historian, he was able to write naval propaganda under the general title of *Foreign Impressions of the Fleet*, subsequently published in book form in 1930, as *The Flower of England's Garland*.

I started my school life at the age of five at King's College, Wandsworth Common, in South London and my father passed on to me my first school report, which indicates that I had made a good beginning. There were only five pupils in my form but somehow I was placed first in all five subjects. A polymath in the making?

I have a few memories of the Great War, although I was only six when it ended. I recall seeing wounded men walking the streets in a medium blue uniform with a bright red tie and I picked up in my road the odd piece of shrapnel, which came from Zeppelin raids on London. This navigable form of balloon, taking to the air in 1908, was felt to have advantages over the aeroplane; behaving well against the wind, it carried fifteen passengers. Raids on London did not amount to much in those war years but for a boy to find a bomb splinter was an interesting experience and these raids were the first effective use of aerial bombardment. Although later one airship disaster followed another, the early use of Zeppelins was an out-

2

standing success. In the six years of their flights before war commenced in 1914, they had carried 35,000 passengers, without mishap.

I remember the Armistice in November 1918 and was taken to Wandsworth Common to see the victory fireworks display. The ghastly horror of the First World War had hardly dawned on a nation overjoyed with the end of hostilities but it gradually became known that from the time the first pistol shot was fired in Sarajevo on 28 June 1914, killing the Archduke Ferdinand, until the guns fell silent in November 1918, over four years later, engulfing almost the whole of Europe and bringing in the USA from April 1917, the loss of life on both sides had been enormous.

In the battle of the Somme tanks were used for the first time and the Allies lost some 600,000, the Germans 650,000. Other later battles produced great carnage; in Passchendaele over 245,000 British losses. It could be said that the flower of youth was mown down in those dreadful years and historians, viewing life as a whole, might well agree that civilization, as it was previously known, would never be the same again.

Life in Edwardian times had been so settled – like an endless summer day, yet ferment was abroad even then. The slippery slope of international imperial rivalry had resulted in the destruction of a life beyond recall. In 1914 twilight was coming on; an evening chill was in the air – in Europe, at least, but perhaps not in the USA. War had done its worst and would continue to do so.

When the Armistice was being signed in 1918, an unknown ex lance corporal in the German Army was recovering in hospital from his war disability. In peacetime he was a house painter and his name was Adolf

Hitler. Devastated to realize that his Fatherland was broken and the German army shattered, he arose to found a revolutionary party and used his tough, visionary oratory to mesmerize the young generation. His Teutonic pride rose to new levels of belief in the all-powerful state and the elimination of all other elements. The success of the Russian Revolution had not passed unnoticed and the huge reparations, which had been demanded of the Germans after the war, were being circumvented by making the Mark valueless. The Versailles Treaty, which arranged peace terms in 1919, was shunned by the Americans but it stripped a defeated enemy of lands, colonies and prestige. Here indeed were the seeds of another world war. We ought not to have been surprised but most of us were. There were limits to which you could subject a defeated nation and these had been breached. What might have been a better way of dealing with a beaten foe would always be open to conjecture.

In 1921, a seemingly insignificant event took place in my young life when I became a member of a Christian youth movement called Crusaders, which, in 2006, celebrates its centenary with a service at the Royal Albert Hall. Later in this book I will go into the details of how this involvement enabled me in the war years to manage life in tented camps and to become, as I believe, a reasonably able commander in the field but at this stage, after a lifetime of involvement in many different ways in the Crusader movement, I occupy an honorary position as one of its vice presidents. More anon.

In 1919, the National Socialist German Workers' party came into being and was led by Adolf Hitler until his suicide in 1945. Almost concurrently, in Italy, the

4

Blackshirts were established under Mussolini and again, as with Hitler, racial superiority was the keynote. Rallies were the life-blood of these almost fanatical uprisings, becoming anti-communist in essence.

Two years after assuming power over his Nazi party Hitler staged an abortive coup against the Bavarian government. It was known as the Munich putsch and the leader suffered imprisonment for his troubles but it gave him the opportunity to write a book that he called *Mein Kampf* (My Struggle). In this work Hitler blamed the Jews for Germany's defeat in the First World War. Thus were the seeds being sown for the extermination of about six million Jews in Hitler's holocaust of 1939-45. It represented approximately two-thirds of European Jewry and they were exterminated in ghastly concentration camps, such as Auschwitz. So much, say many historians, for the nature of European civilization of the twentieth century. How could such a cultivated nation as Germany descend to the depths of annihilation of a whole people? It all started with the end of the Weimar Republic in 1933, crushed under Hitler's jackboot. If ever there was a reason for accepting the Christian doctrine of original sin, this was it.

My father began to make his mark in 1920 as a naval historian through the publication by the Navy Records Society, in two volumes, of the *Life and Works of Sir Henry Mainwaring*. This interesting gentleman was a privateer in Stuart times, a kind of successor to the more famous Tudor, Sir Francis Drake. Piracy, in those days, was a sort of school of seamanship but Sir Henry soon gravitated, in the early seventeenth century, to high command in the Navy and later was appointed Lieutenant of Dover Castle and Deputy Warden of the

Cinque Ports.

These two volumes received outstandingly good reviews, notably from *The Daily Telegraph, The Times Literary Supplement* and *The Observer*. I do not suppose that, at the ages of nine or ten, I helped my father with his literary work but I certainly remember helping him with indexing when I was a young teenager. How I disliked the work, being keener on playing football or cricket on the Common. But I learned that the appearance of these two volumes carried for my father Fellowship of the Royal Historical Society. Many years later, on a visit to the home of Rudyard Kipling at Bateman's, Burwash in Sussex, I surprised the curator in her library by asking if I could handle the two volumes written by my father which I had spotted on the shelves. She almost fell off her chair in amazement. On my own much smaller bookshelves I have one of Kipling's books presented to my father.

My father would, I think, have described himself as an agnostic and in literati terms, he would loosely have identified himself with the giants of his age, George Bernard Shaw (1850-1950) and H. G. Wells (1866-1946), although these two men often disagreed over social and political matters. The whole intellectual climate of the first half of the twentieth century was over-shadowed, initially by Charles Darwin (1809-1882) declaring the natural selection of all living things and then by the era of scientific rationalism headed up by Thomas Huxley (1825-1895) who coined the term agnosticism and violently challenged orthodox theology. As I, even as a very young teenager, was embracing the Christian faith, my father, although not showing active opposition, clearly did not approve of my commitment to what he saw as an outdated religion with, in my case, pietistic overtones of an anti-social nature, all fortunately discarded by me as the years went by. I had inherited an unpleasant sub-culture, which I would describe as life denying rather than life-affirming.

Meanwhile, in the wider world, the competitive status of empire and of impressive armaments continued, notably shown in a rivalry at sea with talk of the necessity for England to outbuild Germany in terms of fighting ships. Suspicion and the fear of war were in the air. The Balkans were, as ever, the cockpit of Europe and, long before the First World War, danger always lurked in that area. In due course, the inevitable resurgence of the German nation came about under the full hypnotic leadership of Hitler and the stage was being set for another cataclysmic conflict. All Europe would become engulfed yet again.

But my father continued his amazing literary output, for his work at the London Library, whilst allowing him to do a certain amount of research, meant that he would always be chasing, at the beck and call of members, volumes in different parts of the library and never getting home on a five and a half day week before about seven o'clock. On his half day he would often be at the British Museum doing his research and all day on Sundays he would be using his typewriter. He never earned more than an annual pay of £300 from the library; his several books, whilst selling well for their type, only added a little to his income, so he often added to that by cataloguing private libraries in London on his half days.

In 1928 my father was appointed the General Editor of *The Seafarers' Library* (Cassell) and he wrote the introduction and notes for the first volume. I think that about six volumes were published but at about the same time he achieved widespread recognition through the publication of a *Bibliography of British Naval History* (Routledge), which became a textbook at naval colleges. Also there was *My Friend the Admiral* (Routledge) and *The Floating Republic* (Bles), the latter also coming out as a Pelican paperback, telling the story of the naval mutiny at the Nore and Spithead in 1797. It was due to be made into a film at a later date but the project never got off the ground. The book was written jointly by Professor Bonamy Dobrée and my father, Dobrée occupying the Chair of English at Leeds University. Other interests of my father included serving on the committee for the preservation of the *Victory* in Portsmouth and on that of the Navy Records Society. I gained the impression that he was very popular with members of the London Library.

In the early 1920s I began to take public examinations, first the Cambridge Junior and then the Cambridge Senior and this study gave rise to one of the great interests of my life – poetry. My special interest became the poets of the First World War and *An Anthology of Modern Verse* (Methuen) contained what was, to my young mind, a significant and most attractive selection. Overlapping with this category of poets were what were known as the Georgians and placing some in alphabetical order I would mention Edmund Blunden, Rupert Brooke (the beau ideal), John Drinkwater, Wilfred Gibson, Robert Graves, Robert Nichols, Wilfred Owen, Siegfried Sassoon, J. C. Squire and Edward Thomas. Those killed or dying in the war, Brooke, Owen and Thomas, achieved a special lustre. It has only recently dawned on me that, in all probability, I may have inherited from my father, a large interest in the overtones and undertones of war. However, my fascination with what was then current poetry extended well beyond the Georgians and the War Poets, notably with regard to three poets who had connections with my father as members of the London Library. These were John Masefield, Poet Laureate from 1930, Sir Henry Newbolt who, my father heard, could well have been in that position had the Conservative government been in power when Robert Bridges died, Masefield being appointed his successor and, in particular, Walter de la Mare with whom, after an introduction to him by my father, I had an on and off relationship for about twenty years. Masefield also had a strong business affinity with my aunt in charge of the receiving desk at the library and almost always sent her some of his verses at Christmas. I visited de la Mare at his house in Taplow, Buckinghamshire for Saturday afternoon tea – an unforgettable and poetry-defining experience.

The scenario for the pre-war and post-world war years would not be complete without reference to the Chamberlains. Joseph (1836-1914) dominated British politics, with an imperialism second only to that displayed in Germany. The English people were securely dominant in India where Queen Victoria had long been Empress, they were established in Egypt and other parts of Africa. It was acknowledged that Britain had the best colonies, much better than the Germans or the Belgians who had the vastness of the Congo for what that was worth. So the rivalry simmered but Kipling warned against the imperialism, 'Lord God of Hosts, be with us yet, lest we forget, lest we forget'. He was not jingoistic!

Late in the 1930s a policy of appeasement, led by Neville Chamberlain (1869-1940) was adopted towards the rising fascist powers. Italy's conquest of Ethiopia in 1925 was greeted by a blind eye and Chamberlain did not want to know about the Spanish Civil War which began in 1936, as a kind of trial run for the fascist powers.

Famously, the disarmament and appeasement advocated in Britain, was typified by Chamberlain and his frequent friendly visits to Hitler culminating in his 1939 message to his country, 'Peace for our time', but the invasion of Czechoslovakia earlier brought about serious doubts of western and British security.

Ten years earlier, a crippling economics crisis gripped the western world. Strangely, Germany's economic plight partly enabled Hitler to achieve his rise to power in the 1930s and in Britain and the US fortunes were lost overnight. Before all this happened, I was enjoying a quiet life at private schools in South London. At Kings College, where few boys stayed on beyond what was called prep-school age, I achieved a significant ambition in becoming a member of the cricket eleven, (three or so members of which were well into their teens) but in 1935, when I was thirteen, my father took me away from Kings College and sent me to a larger private school, Balham Grammar. It was here where I eventually got into the football and cricket elevens, playing against all the other private schools in the area and, most importantly, passed my public examinations, culminating with the London University matriculation at age sixteen. The interesting feature about this kind of private school education is that the system had little or no ability to send its pupils to university. In my own sixth form career only one boy, as I remember, ever went on to university and it seemed that you had either to be very clever or come from a wealthy family to go to Oxford, Cambridge or London. The redbrick universities were hardly on the charts in those days but, in any event, the two private schools which I attended and which had a certain social status did not display any interest in getting their pupils to university. Their social cachet was illustrated by the fact that at

Kings College, bad behaviour outside school hours was so severely dealt with that offenders were no longer allowed to wear the school chocolate coloured velvet cap but, instead, one of serge blue! My personal chagrin at Balham Grammar reached a low point when, my father took me away from school just before my seventeenth birthday to start office work. And I was due to become school cricket captain just after my birthday.

On reflection, I do not think that the era of the small public school, between the wars, had anything to be ashamed of. They encouraged industrious work, took public examinations and boys and girls played competitive sport but this was without much playing field availability. Manners and morality were implied rather than taught but the awful deficiency, as I see it now, was the lack of a following university education. Finally, although the teaching staff often appeared to lack a good qualification, they taught effectively and discipline was not a problem. The headmaster or headmistress owner of a private school was authoritative and without a governing body.

I think it was the spread of state-backed education in the opening of splendid, near-public-school types of senior establishments which proved to be the blow from which privately owned schools never recovered.

I had no choice as to my employment on leaving school. Economic (war) clouds hung over everything but my father had the good fortune, as he rightly thought, to be on good terms with a few of the officials in the next door Clerical Medical and General Life Assurance Society, founded in 1824. The Secretary of the society, Harry Duncan O'Neill, was on the committee of the Library and in April 1929 I went for my maths test and interview at No. 15. I duly started work at £1 a week, raised after a few months to £1. 10s. a week. A junior at the Clerical, as I was, had a list of daily duties but office hours were relatively easy – a quarter to ten until ten to five. My first daily job was to dampen the linen cloths used during the previous day to copy letters in a very antiquated machine in which the copying was achieved by screwing the contraption onto the pages of a book of thin paper. After this came indexing of the previous day's letters, then completing the stamp book and later going on various errands around the office, notably, I recall, taking *The Times* from one departmental head to another. Most of the day was taken up collecting letters from departments for signature by an official. No task was put beyond the office junior – he might be sent round to Fortnum and Mason to buy some exotic delicacy or commissioned to take ice creams round the office for some celebration.

Entry into the service of the Clerical was always considered a privilege as almost all, in the days of the economic crisis, had left public schools, for example Eton, University College School, Merchant Taylors, Malvern, Leys, St Paul's and Wellington. Coming from a minor private school I was fortunate, as was another subsequent entry, whose father had been a batman to one of the directors in the First World War! The Society, as it was sometimes called, was often referred, internally of course, as giving a Bond Street service and the atmosphere was one of refined gentility and leisurely achievement. Heads of departments might spend a large part of their afternoons talking to each other.

The number on the Head Office staff was about fifty, divided into between eight and ten departments, chief among which was the Actuarial Department. The actuarial profession was regarded as the height of mathematical achievement and the early high flyers arrived at

No. 15 with a first class maths degree from Cambridge, afterwards taking another five or so years to attain the coveted distinction of a Fellow of the Institute of Actuaries (F.I.A). I tried my hand at these exams but failed miserably at the first hurdle, so what was left to me as a career prospect? The answer to this question was difficult. There were four or five departments where the head was non-actuarial and only two of these in my time achieved management of the Society. One of these had obtained an accountancy qualification and was made Accountant.

On the evening before news of this was to be sent round to the branches, I was working with him and others on some overtime and I happened to notice, in one of the rooms where we worked, copies of the circular, announcing his appointment. Over supper I could not resist asking him if he knew of his success. He smiled without giving anything away.

Management of the Clerical below board level was commensurate with the staff number – about six. Below General Manager and Actuary, the number two was the Secretary who might come up either through branch management or head office departmental headship, then there were, say, three more junior management, an Assistant Actuary, and Assistant Secretary and, in my time, an Agency Manager responsible for the branches.

To complete the Clerical Medical structural picture, I must mention the outdoor staff. The more outgoing junior members at head office could volunteer to become Inspectors (of Agents) and they were expected to become Branch Managers in due course – notably in the City, West End, Birmingham, Manchester, Leeds etc. So, these were the openings. Half-heartedly I was prepared to join the Inspectors but never got round to it in any realistic way.

Perhaps the saddest and most obvious failures, put back into a minor position on the indoor staff, were those who had failed to make the grade in the outdoor staff at branch level. They had started out volunteering for this more adventurous work but had failed to bring home the bacon, in real terms to generate enough new business from brokers, bank mangers and solicitors in their area.

The Chief Executive of the Society when I joined in 1929 was Arthur Digby Besant, an awesome, remote figure and son of theosophist Annie Besant (1847-1933). My word, she was a capable woman I believe, with atheism, birth control and trades unionism to her credit before going to India to found a Hindu university and sow the seeds for the end of imperialism there. A.D.B. had his own suite of offices, a private luncheon room and staircase. His number two was a much more outgoing personality, Andrew Herrick Rowell, the Assistant Actuary who became President of the Institute of Actuaries in its centenary year and was accordingly knighted. There were a few other actuaries scattered around the office and I remember one very dour head of the actuarial department who had on his staff a brilliant Cambridge graduate and on the day when the young man came to the office with the news that he had passed his finals, was told, 'You know, Kennedy, you can pass too quickly'. The aging actuary who uttered such encouraging words had taken about ten years to qualify. Another actuary for whom I worked said to me, 'You know Manwaring – you like people, I don't'.

Next in importance, departmentally, was the Investments headed by another couple of actuaries, one of whom was a woman and the third member another Cambridge man who, after a few years went into publishing; Morley Fletcher was, I think, his name.

As office junior I was attached to the Renewals Department headed by a substantial figure of a man, who was in charge of about the most boring side of the business, manually preparing and issuing renewal notices and then trying to collect premiums from late-payers. This man had quite a job, looking after five or six juniors, possibly budding actuaries or failed actuaries, and himself becoming the butt of other departmental heads. One of his young men in my time was Eric Tracey who resigned to become ordained in the Anglican Church and later became Bishop of Wakefield. On one occasion Tracey became so exasperated by his boss's continuous prodding that he turned on him with the opening salvo, 'Now, look here, Sutton'. To have answered back so very disrespectfully was to me, understandably horrifying but Eric Tracey by then may well have decided that the Clerical was not for him. He was to become more clerical than the Clerical Medical, which, originally, had offered life assurance cover for the two nominated professions.

The other departments, which filled the front office of No. 15 St James's Square were all three or four strong. These were the cashiers, which claimed me for several of my years, first as number three and then as number two. Initially my chief was Hubert William Burford Rawlings, a charming, eccentric bachelor who was very friendly with the Assistant Secretary of the Society, George Lawton, often referred to as Lord Oxted, where he lived, of course. Rawlings was an organist and choirmaster of Anglo-Catholic persuasion and would often greet me on Monday morning with. 'What did you go round to yesterday', reflecting his love of the processional. Because he lived in the wilds of Sussex he was allowed to arrive at his desk at about 10.15 a.m. and leave us at 4.00

p.m. He always called me 'Marjoribanks' reflecting the strange pronunciation, as he thought, of my name. While I was his number three, he had as his assistant John Charles Wilfred Seex, who had a secret girlfriend who wrote to him at the office. Her unopened letters were always propped up in front of Seex, to be opened later. This annoyed Rawlings.

Each official office letter writer had to initial the typed version before it went in for signature and one day a letter addressed to a Jewish firm was initialled JCWS. The signing official thought this looked like Jews so it had to be retyped etc.

One of my other department stints was writing up the new policy details in what was called, of course, the Order Book and for some years I worked with John Palmer Lloyd who left us to join the regular Army. Several members of the staff, in the 1930s, sensing the need to reinforce the regular services, had joined the Territorial Army. In fact, it might be said that if a member of the staff of the Society did not feel particularly fulfilled by his work at No. 15 – very clerical – he would seek to gain recognition, fulfilment, call it what you will, in service life, sports club leadership, church life or whatever. Another feature of the personnel at No. 15 was that strangely most of the men were either unmarried or childless. Was there some reluctance to become involved which subconsciously persuaded them to take refuge in a safe office job? I wonder.

This much is sure – in the early 1930s three other forms of government – Russian Communism, Italian Fascism and German Hitlerism had little affect either on the lifestyle or on the thoughts of the middle class young men who worked oh, so gently, at No. 15 St James's Square, or in thousands of similar offices. They were, many of

16

them, very occupied with sport – football, rugby, cricket, squash and athletics and every Saturday (only one in about ten off initially), many of them parked their cars outside No. 15, came to work in their sports jackets, grabbed a sandwich brought in by the duty messenger and then set off for Beckenham or Pinner for a great game. The first thing to do on a Monday morning was to tell your chief how many runs you made, how many wickets you had taken or whether you scored a goal. There might have been a blood-bath in 1934, when gangsters of the Nazi party were butchered, Hitler might have engineered the burning of the Reichstag in 1933 or Mussolini had invaded Ethiopia in 1935 but things passed more or less unnoticed by the settled staff of offices in London and elsewhere. Unprepared and unconcerned, the great British people had not awakened yet.

Ramsay MacDonald (1866-1937) became the first Labour Prime Minister in 1924, later being replaced by Stanley Baldwin (1867-1947). Warmongering was a kind of catchphrase in those years and Baldwin encountered much criticism for condoning Italy's annexation of Ethiopia and his apparent reluctance to re-arm in the obvious face of Germany's blatant military build-up. The Peace Pledge Union had many supporters and the continuing advancement of man to become more human under humanism continued to dominate thought and much of the Christian Church. The Oxford Group, later known as Moral Rearmament, under the leadership of the US former Lutheran pastor Frank Buckman (1878-1961) attracted much middle class support. Nothing much could disturb the great British nation while, for example, Germany re-equipped its passenger aircraft as troop carriers. However, by the mid 1930s, young men were all being actively encouraged to join one of the three armed services or the Fire Service, the Special Police or some other public service. I opted for the police – a mistake – donned a uniform and attended lectures at the local Sutton Police Station.

As I reflect on my leisure activities on leaving school and before the start of the Second World War – a period of ten years – I realize that a good deal of my energy and thought was directed towards sport. A report in a local newspaper dealt with my old boys' dinner and was generous enough to state that the old boys' football club, '...was virtually run by R G Manwaring, the Secretary, and a great deal of its success could be traced to his management and energy'. It went on, 'Mr Manwaring was now to undertake the management of the cricket club, and they might be assured that he would make the cricket club pay its own way, as the football club had done'. I notice that, in 1932, the Old Balhamian Cricket Club, with its home ground shared with the London University Athletics Club in Motspur Park, included fixtures against much stronger old boys' sides such as the Old Emanuel and Old Rutlishians also with the London University colleges, Birkbeck and Goldsmiths. In the season 1930 and 1931, I think I played, in a very minor way, for the Mitcham Cricket Club but I cannot quite remember what happened to the Old Boys' Cricket Club, for I joined the prestigious Spencer Cricket Club for the seasons 1933-35, after my family moved to Sutton. I played for Spencer in their minor teams, usually for the third eleven but occasionally for the second, as an opening bowler, once taking seven wickets for forty-two.

My other considerable involvement was in the Crusader movement in which I was elected a group leader for Sutton in 1937. The branch had about 100-120 boys in membership – in those days limited to those from private and public schools, such awful elitism being eliminated later. Apart from helping to run the Sunday afternoon services, I dealt with sporting activities – the occasional football or cricket match and annually participation in the Athletics contest at the London University Ground in Motspur Park to which were also attracted boys from all over the UK. However, my special delight, pre-war, was officiating in one of the camps organized by Crusaders and in January 1939 I received a letter from the Secretary Jack Vereker, who gained a Military Cross in the First World War, asking me if I could take on the duties of Adjutant in August at a camp in Studland Bay, Dorset. I gladly accepted and for about a week assisted in putting up about twenty bell tents, two large marquees, sundry other staff tents and also with the digging of the latrines area. I enjoyed all this, even the digging, and was joined in the work by Donald Wiseman, son of an RAF air commodore and himself to become a group captain in the Second World War before later becoming Professor of Assyriology at London University. I recall that one or two of the other officers brought to camp parts of their TA uniform and had to leave us quite quickly as war became imminent.

My father became very ill in 1939 and died at the age of fifty-seven. In his obituary, *The Times* recorded that he 'never looked his 55 years of age' and went on to state that 'from his unassuming readiness to service the most trivial wants of the most occasional visitor, none would have guessed that Manwaring was a man of learning and much respected authority on certain fields of history'. The notice mentioned the different books that my father had either written or edited and added that he contributed to various Naval periodicals. 'His special study', it went on, 'was the history of the seventeenth century but he knew the eighteenth century almost as well. Members of the Library', the obituary concluded, 'will deeply regret the loss of so generous, courteous and learned a friend and guide.' In an additional notice *The Times* stated that my father was 'a librarian who never failed to surprise anyone who consulted him. He seemed to know the two bulky volumes of the subject index by heart.' *The Daily Telegraph* referred to my father's 'pronounced literary gifts'.

The death of my father left us in a difficult financial situation. He had rented a house in Belmont, Sutton which he was hoping to buy had *The Floating Republic* film been brought to fruition but it became necessary, since he earned little a year from the London Library and there was no death benefit for staff, for us to move to a less expensive rented property. The older of my two younger brothers was planning to get married and the younger was soon to join the RAF so it was left to me, more or less on my own, to look after my mother.

Plans for wartime had been laid in the Clerical Medical and it was announced that No. 15 St James's Square would be more or less evacuated, leaving a skeleton staff to look after the shop with Leslie Abel Westcott, until then an Assistant City Manager, to come and take over responsibility. He was allowed to sign any letter 'for Secretary' but it was noticed that, as the war years went by, the word *for* became less noticeable and, sure enough, soon after the war, he was duly appointed Secretary of the Society.

The remainder of the staff from No. 15 were moved to Beaconsfield in Buckinghamshire, occupying a very pleasant house of medium size, readily converted for office use. Actuaries were, I think, deemed to be a reserved occupation and the younger members of the staff, some of whom were quickly mobilized, were naturally regarded as being due for national service. A frequent communication was arranged giving delivery of papers between St James's Square and Beaconsfield and so the scene was set for a very limited wartime style of business. During my service with the RAF I only visited Beaconsfield once and was taken to lunch in a small local restaurant by Norman Lewis Carey, a Joint Secretary, who introduced me to one of the waitresses as 'one of my boys'.

So, on 3 September 1939 Britain was at war. Hitler had organized, re-equipped and led a defeated nation but now he had gone a step too far. In 1934 he became the Führer, head of the old Weimar Republic. He very cleverly devalued his currency to avoid paying proper reparations and in 1923 it needed many millions of German marks to buy a sovereign, a pram full to purchase a loaf of bread and the nation was to be purified by exterminating the Jewish people. So far they had turned their backs on the Christian faith that, on his seventieth birthday in 1935, Ludendorff (1865-1937), a German general in the First World War, who was by then a Nazi, declared, 'We Germans are the people which has freed itself furthest from the teaching of Christianity'. The crimes of the mid 1930s, butchering of enemies, burning of the Reichstag etc. were likened to those at the end of the Roman Empire in the third century, Rome having held European life together until then. The Führer, in final breach of the Versailles Treaty, introduced conscription in 1935 and the faithful went wild with delight. With every roar of the Nazi tiger, the smaller nations quaked. Questions would forever plague the civilized world as to why it all happened but Hitler had marched on, hoodwinking the rest of Europe by annexing Austria in 1938, his *Anschluss* producing what he called a united country; then the final throw of the dice when he stepped into Poland and we, the British people, along with the French, were at war with Germany. After about six years of an all-embracing conflict, human losses were unbelievable.

<u>Combatants</u>

Germany	3,500,000
UK	264,443
Soviets	11,000,000
Japan	1,300,000
USA	292,131
Total	16,356,574

<u>Civilians</u>

Germany	780,000
	(59,300 from RAF bombs)
UK	92,673
	(61,000 from bombing)
Soviets	7,000,000
Japan	672,000
USA	6,000
In concentration camps Jews	5,700,000
Total	14,250,673

An amazing fact of the Second World War – about the same number of civilians perished as those in the armed forces. 'Man's inhumanity to man makes countless thousands mourn' wrote Robert Burns in the eighteenth century. His estimate was very much an understatement – there were millions rather than thousands.

This terrible end product was to be the backdrop to the next six years and I now propose to chronicle my path to war in the Far East.

The Enchanted Lake - Wandsworth Common

One day the rustic bridge came down
And they built a safer one of stone,
With disenchantment in a world
Where childhood kept the feast alone.

We fished the edge or weedy depths,
Bright stickleback or minnow found -
In summers when the lake was dry
We trod upon forbidden ground.

We watched the rhododendrons blaze
And swans desert their lofty nest,
With coots and moorhens hurrying,
By leaves and osiered banks caressed.

A half-sunk punt moored by the bridge,
Grown old in slime and gossamer,
Once crossed to the island sanctuary
When Ulysses sailed to Ithaca.

Randle Manwaring

Old Couples on Trains

Not much to say - all has been said
and said a thousand times before.
They quietly pass the hours, in thought
recalling other railway trips
made in leisurely days of steam.

The landscape is still green, the corn
is ripe, farmhouses almost unchanged,
more cars in car parks everywhere,
high flats in country towns - these things
must go unsaid on the Inter-City train.

Remembering how young people travel
across the world by more exciting means,
they wonder where it all will end,
as minds fall back through fifty years
to joys on the London, Brighton, South Coast line.

Randle Manwaring

Private School, 1925

A private school - before the State took over -
where few stayed on beyond the thirteen stage
and those who did became, at once young despots
in a genteel, adolescent world.

The masters, graduates who had lost their way,
maintained, in style, their middle-class prestige;
they biffed the dunderheads about the ears
or stood them up before the form.

For little enough a term, this education,
mirroring the tinsel values of the times,
gave its badge - a chocolate coloured velvet cap
trimmed with a ribbon of shining gold.

The Head, always in authoritarian gown,
wielded, most subtly, a power of life and death,
his ultimate in sanctions a plain blue cap
for boys he sent to Coventry.

Obedience came by fear of a knobkerrie
or the cane or missiles flung or sarcasm;
all pin-pricks compared with the sentence of social death -
the surge of deepest opprobrium.

Randle Manwaring

Chapter 2

Training for Overseas

I did not enjoy my time as a special police constable during the year I spent working out of a local headquarters in Cheam Park. We did two months' daytime duty and then one month on nights. During the day, duties could include checking on minor offences or trying to track down burglars, always with the help of the Regulars; we also controlled school crossings. At night, blackout regulations had to be enforced – a very tedious business – and bombing alerts dealt with by ushering people into large air-raid shelters. To start with, sleeping by day, after night duty, was difficult and, as a result, one had to keep inconvenient hours, making it difficult to have much social life.

It is, I think, hardly surprising that, almost immediately following the outbreak of war, I joined the Royal Air Force Volunteer Reserve and volunteered to become a wireless operator. I often wonder why I decided to muster in this trade for I was never one for the more technical side of things and feel quite sure I would have disliked the wireless operator training and the work as much as I disliked being a policeman. However, the war in Europe had gone devastatingly badly for the Allies in those early months; Belgium was overrun and the outlook was bleak. The Government decided to take airfield defence seriously and so, in the summer of 1940, it was decided to call up all and sundry into a new category of airman entitled Ground Gunner. I was one of those so called up and reported for duty in Blackpool. There, I donned the uniform of a second class aircraftsman and was billeted on one of those famous motherly landladies, who cared for three or four of us young men and, memorably, produced high tea as the evening meal. This was dominated, in my mind by the cake stand on the middle of the table and food, in the main, was just about enough to satisfy the appetites of us twenty-somethings who had been square-bashing most of the day on Blackpool Front. I recall that there was a large number of short Polish airmen, equally under the commanding culture of the drill sergeants, for only a few months earlier their country had been completely overrun by the Nazis.

Another feature of Blackpool which I remember is a lecture in the ballroom where a regular squadron leader addressed a few hundred of us on the subject of security in the RAF and as he walked up and down the stage in a theatrical style, he warned us, turning threateningly towards us, that he had known men shot for giving away secret information, so we had better be careful what we said or did.

After a couple of weeks initial training but so far no experience of firing a rifle we were paraded and invited to state a preference for an airfield posting. Naturally, most of us asked for a location close to home but I doubt if anyone was successful in that regard and I was sent to a newly built airfield north of Norwich, called Horsham St

Faith. There were no beds available, mattresses and blankets only; I slept on the floor next to a contemporary from Wolverhampton who greeted us with, 'Where chcow cum from?' Sadly, he was completely illiterate and when letters arrived from his girlfriend one of us had to read them to him. Similarly, we wrote letters from him to her and, naturally, enjoyed being of some help in a situation entirely new to us. My mate also amazed me by sleeping in his RAF shirt with the collar detached.

At Horsham St Faith, ground defence began to take shape. There were machine-gun positions around the perimeter where Lewis guns were put at the ready and we were given basic instructions on loading, 'number one stoppages' - whatever they were. Because of my peacetime office life, I was given one or two cushy clerical jobs writing out passes, late night or sleeping-out and also for a long while I was positioned on the watch tower of the airfield without any anti-aircraft weapon but presumably to spot enemy aircraft.

For my time off, I visited nearby Norwich and fell in with a small local branch of Crusaders where one of the seniors invited me to tea with his family. There I fell in love with his sister, Betty Rout, then aged twenty and so the whole course of my life was altered. We became engaged on her twenty-first birthday and married just about a year after I had joined up. My stay at Horsham St Faith did not last all that long however and I think my next posting was to Eglinton in Northern Ireland. At that stage I was promoted to the rank of corporal but decided, on returning to Norfolk for the wedding, to get married in mufti rather than in uniform. At an earlier stage – I cannot remember exactly when – I applied for a commission and was called to the Air Ministry for an interview where I had the good fortune to find that one of the members of the selection board played cricket for Esher and against whom I must have played pre-war.

At Eglinton, we were busy putting up barbed wire defences around the airfield and became quite skilful at handling that unmanageable commodity. In nearby Londonderry, feelings against the English were unmistakable. In a village post office nearby, I commented to a lady that the weather had been so bad but I hoped the crops were not being affected. 'Not the weather', she countered, 'but they would be since the British were here'. And walking in Londonderry in uniform it was not unusual for boys to shout at you 'Dirty British'.

My wife and I went to Eastbourne on the briefest of honeymoons only to be summoned to report to my unit which had then been posted for further training to the Royal Enniskillen Fusiliers at Omagh in County Tyrone. No sooner there than Corporal Manwaring was instructed to report immediately to the Army Officer Cadet Training Unit in Douglas in the Isle of Man. This was, I believe, a three months' course and gave us simulated combat training, more drill, of course and firing guns on ranges. I was allowed to have my wife stay at a Douglas Hotel so life was very bearable. We had some unarmed combat, bayonet fighting practice (which I loathed) and the more peaceful Tactical Exercises Without Troops (TEWTs for short) but although I fancied myself as being good at drill, I do not think I matched up at all well with the requirement of OCTU and overall my officer in charge informed me that I had only done moderately well.

Back to Eglington where I went as a junior officer and quite soon I was posted back to England - Norfolk in fact and so my wife returned to her home. I was posted to West Raynham, a light bomber station where the commanding officer was Group Captain the Earl of Bandon, sometimes irreverently referred to as the 'Abandoned Earl!'

The loss of Crete to the Germans in 1941 was the catalyst for bringing to high command the vulnerability of airfields to attack and loss and may well have been the moment of conception for the RAF Regiment, founded in 1942. There is little doubt that the airborne invasion of Crete – the first ever on a large scale – made everyone aware of the liability of an occupying force to sudden, deadly attack from the skies. Some purists thought the Regiment a luxury and others called it Churchill's private army so I suppose it might in some way have been a bright idea of his. However, Ground Defence became the RAF Regiment and I had the honour to be one of its founding officers. The particular Regiment Squadron to which I was posted was at West Raynham but I was sent to the satellite at Massingham with a detachment of Regiment personnel and once again we were armed with Lewis machine guns posted round the perimeter. An army unit was in charge of the heavier anti-aircraft guns and I had the privilege of using their officers' mess but I was actually billeted on the local doctor, by the name of Appleton, where I was given a room at the top of the house with no hot water. Every morning Mrs Appleton kindly brought me water for shaving. Her husband was a gentle and kindly doctor whose dispensary was coloured by red and green bottles seen from the exterior. He once told me that after a number of patients had their ills dealt with by a bottle of what he called out to his dispenser as ADT, he was asked what this stood for and informed his enquirer 'any damned thing'.

One of the pleasures of being stationed at Massingham was a mild friendship with the Birkbeck family. They

31

occupied the largest house in the village and the occupants; Colonel Birkbeck and Lady Joan Birkbeck were kind enough to befriend this young officer. I was invited to have baths at their house, none being available to me at the Appletons and their young daughter Mary, aged about ten or eleven and I established a happy rapport. The Birkbecks were part of Sandringham society and occasionally I was taken by them on family picnics there.

Being at Massingham had another distinct advantage - I could go to Norwich at weekends to spend them with my wife and I travelled to and from on what was, the now extinct, West Norfolk railway line. It went through, I think, to Kings Lynn and I used to take the train from and to Fakenham, not far from Massingham. Returning to duty one very foggy morning the train emptied at Melton Constable and the guard contended that he could not go any further. It happened I was to attend a Monday morning parade at West Raynham so I remonstrated with the guard that he really must go on to Fakenham. After a fair amount of persuasion he agreed and all was well. I was the only passenger. Sometimes I had a visit at Massingham from Paddy Bandon (he was an Irish peer) and he would drive me round the perimeter inspecting my unit. On one occasion, he encountered a fox in our path and chased it accordingly.

In my time as a junior officer at West Raynham and Massingham I was often chosen to attend the various courses on offer and one of the most enjoyable took me back to Douglas in the Isle of Man, the subject being aircraft recognition. This very much appealed to me and it emphasized the necessity, for example, of distinguishing momentarily between one of our own aircraft, for example a Hurricane or a Spitfire and an enemy

Messerschmitt or Focke Wulf fighter. Head on it was quite a problem. Unlike my UCTU, I came top of this course but I never personally used my new ability. Another course, of a totally different nature, was run by the Army and was called the Junior Leader's Course. This involved sleeping under hedges at night, crawling from one hideout to another and generally simulating combat conditions. A camouflage course in Norwich, again run by the Army, was pleasant and quite academic, run by a well-known actor whose name I forget. But undoubtedly, the most peculiar course I went on was that for the Parachute and Cable Unit which was a clever method for airfield defence but I very much doubt whether it was ever used. These units were situated round an airfield perimeter, they looked like Roman candle fireworks and, when let off, sent up a defensive line each supporting a parachute. But I have nearly forgotten what was, probably for me, the most important course. It was held on the coast in the Newcastle area and instructed us in the use of the Bofors light anti-aircraft gun, which became standard equipment in many of the Regiment units. It always surprised me that, whether we were learning about PAC rockets or shells fired by the Bofor gun, we were always expected to master the internal intricacies of the missiles and draw pictures of all the details.

I must not forget, in remembering courses preparing as for battle, that the most frightening was on Salisbury plain where the Army fired live ammunition landing a few yards ahead of us as we crawled slowly towards it. We all survived.

My daughter, Rosemary, was born in 1942 and the Birkbecks kindly offered the use of their lodge for the young family. They said that my great personal successes in the village were with the Rector and their daughter Mary. But the time was coming for the next move and I was posted to an American Air Base in Norfolk at Hethel. There I was the only RAF officer and benefited greatly from participation in the goodies which were part and parcel of overseas duty for the Americans. I remember the lovely towels which were available from the PX, also supplies of chocolate not on sale in the UK. I cycled from Hethel to visit Betty and Rosemary, who were living with my in-laws at the time. Incidentally, I might mention that it was obligatory for every RAF officer to be able to ride a bike, a motorbike and to be able to drive a 5-ton truck.

Another very interesting posting came my way in 1942, by which time I had become a squadron leader. Change was in the air and the Americans were everywhere. I was sent to Middle Wallop in Hampshire, a delightful spot with a charming musical suite to its credit – the Wallops – Middle, Over and Nether – by Eric Coates. I think my service there was, for some reason quite brief for the important airfield was to be handed over to the Americans and a mess party was held to dispose of all the mess funds in one night. What a party! Lobsters and crabs were flown in from Cornwall and everyone was invited, including all the Army units for miles around. For a while, Betty and Rosemary lived at Nether Wallop and it was there that Rosemary took her first steps. My most abiding memory of the party was an unexpected link-up with the head of my department at the Clerical Medical at the outbreak of war. His name was John Brook Williams and could fairly be described as the archetypical Territorial Army Officer. He exuded discipline, formality, commitment and zest and had gone away from the office a week or so before the war had actually started. In a pencil written letter to me he said:

(Somewhere in Essex, Thursday).

My dear Manwaring,

So sorry to have to had to leave you in such a hurry. We are at present living in an empty house miles from anywhere sleeping on the floor and only stew and bully beef to eat. If all the trouble fizzled out I should be back at St James's Square by the end of next week. Please remember me to all at No 15.

Yours ever,
J B Williams

(The postmark on the letter was Southend on Sea!)

Williams was often called J.B. and I was his number two in the Underwriting Department. We prepared cases for underwriting and collected medical reports accordingly. Once a year I did an interesting analysis of the previous year's causes of death. I recall finding that, year after year, the causes of death among our policyholders remained more or less the same - from memory, it was forty per cent from cancer, forty per cent from heart disease and the remaining twenty per cent divided between suicide, accidents and lesser causes. Just occasionally, an interesting death was recorded, for example 'encephalitis lethargica in Guatemala, body never found'.

Discussing medical evidence with our medical directors was often quite interesting, for example using the height and weight tables (age related), I showed an underweight case to Sir Arnold Stott, then chief physician at, I think,

Westminster Hospital and, after some discussion, Sir Arnold commented 'What's wrong with being a little underweight anyway, I certainly am'. Another very eminent medical man on the board of the Clerical in my day was Lord Moynihan who, we were told, had three ambitions in the 1930s, viz, a seat in the House of Lords, President of the Royal College of Surgeons and an annual income of £10,000, which seems very small today. He achieved all three.

Another leading medical man was Dr Edward Revel Cullinan (Lord Horder's son-in-law). Someone joked that we were not to hold this against him. He came to us from Bart's and I once asked him whether he thought a friend of mine at Bart's, who became Dean, would ever get a knighthood and he answered, 'Not unless one of the Royal Children suffers from bed-wetting and then he might'. I knew that my friend was a distinguished surgeon but I hadn't previously realized that he had this extra knowledge. When I visited him many years later, in a nursing home, he told me how very disappointed he was with his profession, for they could not discover what was really wrong with him but, in the same breath, he told me he suffered from mitral stenosis, depression and constipation.

Sir Heneage Ogilvie, a surgeon and Sir John Rose Bratford (a physician), are other names which come to mind but I once had the pleasure of visiting, at his home in Langham Place in the West End, Sir Percival Horton-Smith Hartley, another director. He had conducted an interesting appraisal into the longevity of university oarsmen. I think he may have been one himself. In general, when a potential policyholder with a borderline medical situation came to St James's Square for an examination by one of our medical directors, everything had to be carefully prepared, the room, the paperwork and the messenger (then so called) who would stand guard for the proceedings.

Of course J.B. did not return from Southend, as he thought he might and I was able to follow the wartime career of this peacetime TA major until – would you believe it – we found ourselves standing next to each other in the loo, during this grand Middle Wallop party. I was by then in his equivalent rank and his amazement was such that, noticing me by his side he exclaimed: 'Manwaring, the war has made a man of you.' Such had been his implied opinion of me, after some hesitation, when I joined the Police Force in 1937.

About this time, I had another very interesting posting – to Feltwell, just into Suffolk where the Station Commander was Group Captain Kippenberger, a New Zealander. The station was occupied by two squadrons of light bombers – one Australian and one New Zealand. Appropriately, the chaplain was also a New Zealander with strong Australian connections – Dr Stuart Barton Babbage. He and I became close friends and I found him to be the most exemplary padre – at one with the air crews who almost daily faced death and generally making himself known and respected in the RAF community. He sometimes flew with the aircrew to get the feeling and just once, at a riotous mess party, they actually de-bagged him at some unearthly hour. On the high mess ceiling there were impressions of human bottoms left in soot, tables having been placed one upon another to achieve the marks! Nothing was thought beyond the scope of these men, off duty, who did not know when they might perish. Once one rode on a motorbike down the corridors of the officers' mess.

Stuart Babbage was a man of great initiatives. When

the great Christian writer, C. S. Lewis was at the height of his fame, Stuart was able to persuade him to come and preach at Feltwell and, on another occasion, this innovative chaplain took a coach party to attend the famous Nine Lessons and Carols service at Kings College Chapel, Cambridge. To my lasting regret, I did not give Stuart the support I might have done and which he deserved, for often, at weekends, I would be off to Norwich to see my wife and young daughter, thus missing C. S. Lewis etc.

Stuart became engaged to the 'Queen Bee' (the senior WAAF officer) at Feltwell and the wedding took place in the village church with the New Zealand High Commissioner gracing the occasion with his presence. A young officer friend of Stuart's was best man and I was one of the guests. After the war, I did my best to keep in touch with Stuart who went on to become, successively Dean of Sydney and Dean of Melbourne, also head of an Australian College. He continued being a man of out-standing ability and courage and ought to have been elected a Bishop in Australia but I fear he was too outspoken and too much the individual to fit neatly into an episcopal mould. We met on the two occasions post war when my eldest son worked in Sydney and in 2004 he published his *Memoirs of a Loose Canon*.

After Feltwell, things were on the move for the opening of a second front in Europe and units of the RAF Regiment were being trained for that purpose, shuffling around the country waiting for things to happen. At one stage there were mock-up landing craft in which we practised different manoeuvres with heavy vehicles but then, as a vast invasion force was being assembled in southern England, my unit was being ushered into a position of readiness for action. It seemed that in 1943 and 1944, the units for which I was responsible were always being moved around in the south and once my squadron was merged with another unit. This meant a farewell parade ceremony at which I was presented with a Bible inscribed 'In memory of service together 1943 and 1944'. It was signed by most of the senior NCOs and headed by our warrant officer, WO Piggott. Other signatories were Flight Sergeants Askam and McColl, Sergeants Quinn, Fletcher and Jenkins. I was amazed and still am that they thought this to be an appropriate presentation for, as far as I know, I never had the opportunity of declaring my Christian faith and naturally wondered what clues I had given.

One of the more unusual assignments given to my squadron and in no way connected with an airfield, was when, presumably, in augmentation of Army AA units, we were given the task of providing AA defence against low-flying enemy aircraft attacking coastal towns. Accordingly one of the flights in the squadron was located at Folkestone, one at Ramsgate and one at Margate with headquarters at Pegwell Bay. We heard the guns from across the Channel loosing off against the south but from then on there were no enemy aircraft to deal with.

Three other 1943/44 moves came to mind, both made in terms of waiting for the second front, wondering if my own unit would be required. One was to Davidstow Moor in Cornwall, rather a long way from the main troop build-up in the south, then to Upottery in Devon where we felt we were closer. The longest but yet brief spell, marking time, was at Penclaud near Swansea in South Wales where the unit was squashed into a hutted camp. I particularly remember departure of the unit by train from Swansea with a large number of our local friends coming to say good-bye and, as this included a group of young ladies, I wondered what responsibility I might have for the men leaving broken romances or worse behind as we moved on.

One of the features of the development of the RAF Regiment in the early days was the appointment of what were called Group Defence Officers. One of these gentleman, probably a captain or a major in the First World War, was appointed to each airfield and naturally continued to wear army uniform. Their duties included advice on airfield defence and, I think, keeping an eye on the burgeoning Regiment. Inevitably, some of these very middle-aged gentlemen were rather blimpish, Poona-wallah types but they had a difficult job, in which they became surplus to requirements in due course.

It gradually became clear, that, despite my unit's lining up in the south of England we were not required in the invasion of Europe. So what next? At this stage I recall that, when it became clear, we were to go to the Far East, I, along with other Squadron Commanders, was summoned to the RAF Records Office in Gloucester where we were able to nominate any members of the unit whom we thought unsuitable for service in, presumably Burma. This presented us with difficult choices for, inevitably, in a unit of 200 – 300 men, there were those who chose to express their personalities. Naturally, from those in the unit who most often reported sick, I chose to de-select most, realizing that they might have an extra problem in a country where malaria, dysentery and typhoid occurred quite often. In addition, those who were in any way troublesome in this country were more than likely to be troublesome when the going got difficult and these I nominated for further UK service. (Anyone over the age of say thirty-five, as it turned out, was unlikely to survive in Burma.) The officers all had rigid medicals and, despite a tendency to varicose veins, I was pronounced fit. I am quite sure that most members of the unit eagerly looked forward to overseas service, for they had waited a long time to see any action. For myself I had only one thought – leaving my wife and family, David, my second child, having been born recently.

During the summer of 1944, I had enjoyed the occasional game of cricket, notably, as I gladly recall, one on the Somerset County Ground at Taunton where the squadron raised a team through the influence of Arthur Jepson, one of my sergeants who, in peacetime, opened the bowling for Nottinghamshire. He and I opened the attack in this side and the game became quite a landmark in my memory. Arthur was a pleasant enough man, he often got time off to go and keep goal for Port Vale and, one way and another, I deemed him surplus to requirements for Burma. In the post-war years he became a first-class umpire and I sometimes had a drink with him after a game on the County Ground at Hove but I never had the courage to tell him that, presumably I did him a favour by not taking him to the Far East. I think, but cannot be sure, that he would have been quite grateful.

Another unusual feature of squadron life was that once we had our own band and, looking back, I find it interesting that from about 300 men there were at least half a dozen instrumentalists. At the same time I was informed that the squadron had its own group of capable peacetime burglars who had all brought their equipment with them but they managed to keep their activities secret.

With the stage being set for overseas posting we were all given a briefing, at officer level, of what life abroad and in action would be like. The speakers were two or three

41

Group Defence Officers, all of whom would be able to call on their experience overseas. Being such a keen cricketer and with the Taunton memory fresh in mind I asked the question as to whether it was thought worthwhile for me to take my cricket bag. 'Oh yes', was the reply, 'you should be able to get a few games as you pass through India'. Accordingly, I packed my cricket bag, appropriately marking it 'Not wanted on voyage' but that was the last I saw of my gear for, when unloaded at Bombay, it must have taken the fancy of some young cricketer and so used to further the talents of Indian enthusiasts. I am, I think, proud of that.

At that point I was in charge of No. 2743 Squadron and we sailed from Liverpool late in 1944 in a remarkable convoy of converted pleasure liners. We were assigned to the *Queen of Bermuda*, often referred to as the 'Queen of Blue Murder' and I fear that the sleeping conditions for other ranks were rather rudimentary. However, there were about six or eight troop ships, all under the watchful, circling care of protecting destroyers, with Liberator aircraft watching from the skies. It must have been an impressive sight and we kept clear of U-boat attacks on the long journey, via the Suez Canal to Bombay. A large part of our time seemed to be spent wearing our life jackets but there was still plenty of time for socializing, particularly as there were a number of WAAF officers on board. The nights with the phosphorescent illumination of the sea were very impressive and, one couple, meeting on embarkation, were engaged by the time they reached Bombay!

However, I reached a low point of my career as an officer when, about half way through the voyage, the Squadron Warrant Officer came to see me, ostensibly to enquire about my own well-being but in reality to express the Squadron's regret that they had seen nothing of me on the voyage to date. I shall never forget my feeling of shame but for me I must have been so enchanted by life on board that I quite overlooked my prime responsibility as Squadron Commander.

Convoy, 1944

Suddenly we felt the kind soft air
Blowing across the sea
And there was laughter everywhere;
Spent then the storm and turned to fair
Was the changeling world to me.

Over the waves where the dark must shroud
Great ships in the tropic night
The moon from her space beneath a cloud
Flecks silver the waves and spume is endowed
With phosphorescent light.

After much easting with Africa nigh
Offshore all captains must wait;
While feluccas unfurl against the sky,
Brown skins, red capped, are passers-by
And all pass through the orient gate.

Randle Manwaring

Embarkation Leave, 1944

Back from the strong and tireless arms
Of wife and children, now must go
The soldier sworn to victory;
He feels awhile their love and warms
His heart, which soon must overflow
With tears that none could ever see.

In these bright, scurrying days he felt
A peace unsullied by the strife -
Forgotten are those marching feet -
And here the unfettered spirit dwelt
To learn again the art of life,
In war's surcease, a bitter sweet.

Now to the fight where nations fall
Headlong across the eastern sea,
The warrior goes without a name;
Hears in the distance many a call
Sent from a global threnody
And answering sails, with the world aflame.

Randle Manwaring

Whither

When the flickering present lies grey in ashes
And her gipsying years are a county away,
Will they remember this straggling encampment's
Discordant sounds at the close of a day?

They will have built, in the fields, to-morrow,
Towns for their trading and a road to the sea
Where the romany children will sing together
Or burn to death by a blistered tree.

Randle Manwaring

Chapter 3

Road to Rangoon

Disembarking at Bombay, we were briefly housed in a transit camp and then sent across India by train. Why not by air, I cannot imagine, for the Jungle Training School run by the Army in Bengal was, I remember, accessible by air, since after our training, we flew from a nearby airstrip into the war zone. This train journey lasted for a whole week, the experience being unforgettable. How we were provisioned for the length of time escapes my memory but I certainly recall the distance travelled, via Poona and Secunderabad, the latter place being the home of the RAF Regiment in the Far East. But we did not stop anywhere for long and I estimate that the journey was between 1,000 and 2,000 miles. It must have been a trial for us all but we survived. I recollect that we were often sent off into sidings, which was useful for stretching our legs and sometimes we were entertained by a snake charmer with his cobra. Otherwise, the local *char wallahs* would be there to sell us tea. I cannot now recall whether 2743 Squadron was the only one on board but it was definitely the longest, slowest train journey I have ever experienced.

So, we arrived in Bengal, subsequently as a country split up in the India/Pakistan settlement and were instructed by the Army as to how to survive in Burma, either in traditional jungle or on the torrid plains. Everyone was recovering from the monsoon or longing for the next one. On one night exercise we experienced what you might call a tiger alert and snatched some sleep in our vehicles. But the most lasting memory of that period of further training was over a river crossing exercise, badly researched by the instructors. A volunteer swimmer was called for and Leading Aircraftsman Jones stepped forward. The theory was that some string was fastened around his waist, followed by some heavier cord and then, progressively stronger rope, until the final attachment was very heavy indeed. The weight pulled LAC Jones down to his death. I was disgusted by the tragedy, for he volunteered as a strong swimmer and the Army unit were very much to blame for mounting the fatal exercise without proper research. The next day the funeral of a very popular member of the squadron was accompanied by singing the Welsh hymn *Guide me O Thou Great Jehovah*.

So we moved on to our first posting in the war zone, the whole unit, including equipment, flown in commando type aircraft. My unit, 2743 Squadron, was one of thirteen arriving for duty in south-east Asia at the beginning of 1945 – four light anti-aircraft units and nine Field Squadrons – a total of ten wings all passing through Agartala en route for airfields in central Burma. The Regiment had been used in defending airfields against enemy attack from the air but now, as in other theatres of war, occupying successfully, airfields, in support of the general Army led advance, was the order of the day. Our own experience going forward significantly, showed the way in which the war was progressing as the Japanese were being driven out of Burma. The front line was more often than not difficult to define and often Japanese units would find themselves left behind in jungle conditions to attack the British forces in the rear of their advance. The Royal Engineers did a marvellous job in constructing new runways with interlocking metal strips and, on many occasions after I was put in charge of a Wing, the Wing Commander (Flying) and I would put on our parachutes, jump into a two-seater Piper Cub aircraft and he would pilot us forward to the next airfield, testing its suitability for our joint occupation. After one trip which I believe had its own minor hazards, we stepped out of the aircraft, had a congratulatory handshake, on which he enquired, 'Are you one?' I must have given a kind of Freemason greeting for I countered, 'No, that deformed little finger is the result of my misjudging a steepling catch in the field during a game of cricket in, I think 1936' (Sutton v Wimbledon).

During an earlier time, before my promotion, I had a very anxious time on the forward airstrips, never quite knowing how far we were from action. The aircraft used by the squadrons were mainly Hurribombers (converted Hurricane fighters), as they were called and they carried one bomb under each wing. If, as happened once as I watched the aircraft returning, a bomb got caught up, failing to be released, the landing produced a fatal result as the exploding bomb sent the pilot to his death. I lost a very dear friend in these conditions. In the evening before he had entertained me on his guitar. He seemed to know he was soon to meet his death. He was buried the next day.

We flew into Schwebo, also Sinthe, in the Mandalay area and we witnessed the fall of that great city, under heavy bombardment, in the spring of 1945. We had stopped off briefly at Ondaw and on most of these airstrips I was able to conduct the occasional Sunday evening service for those not on duty. I had taken overseas with me a hip-pocket size, zip-up Bible from which I read a lesson, and also about 100 printed hymn sheets. Years later, an article about me in the very popular glossy magazine, *This England*, prompted one of my former colleagues in 2743 Squadron to write to me as follows:

> It has been a long, long time since you and I met but I have never forgotten you; for the kindness and goodness shown to us young RAF Regiment Airmen in 1944/45.

The Battle of Meiktila, lasting for three weeks, took place in March 1945 and the Regiment was heroically led by Wing Commander Max Lander who, with nearly all the officers under his command, was killed in the conflict. The units had only just flown in from Agartala and were in action after only two days.

My wartime colleague continued his letter to me:

> Reference was, made to 2708 Squadron getting a bashing at Meiktila and that we were the next Squadron to move forward. But the sadder news for us was that you had been promoted to Wing Commander and was going to Wing HQ. Our hearts sank as we looked up to you to lead us through the Campaign and home.
>
> I still talk about how you used to have a Sunday service. All of us sat round and you read the scriptures to us, and a Cpl Halliday, who was a

Salvationist, led the hymns, and how LAC Jackson, chef, used to bake little cookies in his field oven and we all had tea and cookies after you gave us the news from the European front.

He concluded:

The last time you and I had conversation was when you were recruiting for the RAF Regiment Para Squadron and you interviewed me at Rangoon. I did join 2810 Para Squadron under Squadron Leader D. C. Sullivan. When we assembled at Begarpit, near Secunderabad to join 2810 we were a trifle apprehensive as to who our CO was to be! Remembering him as a Flight Lieutenant in Agaratla we thought we were in for a rough time, but he turned out to be as nearly as good and kind as you!So God bless you, for all you have been and done for us.

What an affirmation of the worth of doing the wartime work of leading a squadron of the Regiment (or whatever).

By May we were quickly on the move through Magwe and Myingyan. The climate in central Burma before the monsoon was very hot but only the younger men, speaking generally, kept free from minor health problems; a number were not so minor and had to return to the UK. We called dysentery 'squitters' in its early stages and I once recorded in my diary 'LAC Barkess - 10 times sick in two months'. However, the occasional visit from an ENSA concert party helped to keep up our spirits but *they* had to be entertained!

At one stage in our airfield occupancy, we were advised

to dig in and sleep below ground level since air raids from the retreating enemy were expected. In another location, my bed above ground was found to be over a nest of pythons so I had to be moved quickly!

Recruiting men for the one and only Regiment Para Squadron was given to me by headquarters in Kandy so I went round the different units in south-east Asia interviewing volunteers and I well remember that there was no shortage. However, although the unit went into arduous training it was never used, for VJ Day in August intervened. Later, Squadron Leader Sullivan, the CO, was promoted and given command of the Depot in Secunderbad with the rank of Group Captain. He was a born leader.

During the height of the campaign in Burma we had a visit from Group Captain Jack Harris, our commanding officer. He came to see as many wings as possible and was in the process of selecting his No. 2 as a wing commander in Kandy, Ceylon, and he invited me to join him in this vacant position (as it were 'on appro'). I viewed this as an exciting prospect – the life of a staff officer in such beautiful surroundings was most appealing, so off I went in high hopes, hardly expecting to see much of Burma in the future. I certainly found the living and working conditions most agreeable - the sight of pineapples growing wild by the roadside was something which I shall not forget and which seemed to epitomize Kandy.

I think I stayed for two weeks as the Group Captain's No. 2 and enjoyed attending the daily conference of Air Marshal Sir Keith Park. On going to the first of those, my chief said to me 'Now remember this is not your opportunity for making your maiden speech from the floor of the house'. I do not know whether my chief

1. The school cricket team. Randle Manwaring on the left in the back row.

2. Battle of Meiktila, 1945. *Painting by Frank Wootton, by courtesy of Peter Livanos.*

3. Wing Commander Randle Manwaring, RAF Regiment, 1945.

4a and 4b. Japanese generals surrendering in Rangoon, 1945.

5. John Masefield, Poet Laureate, a friend of the family, in 1951.

7. Wellesley hockey team, 1961.

8. Randle Manwaring on his first directorship, 1964.

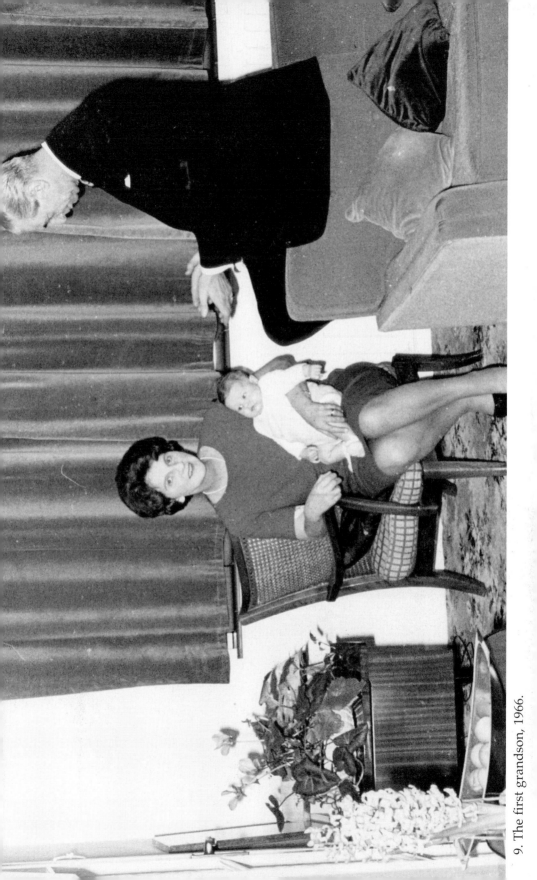

9. The first grandson, 1966.

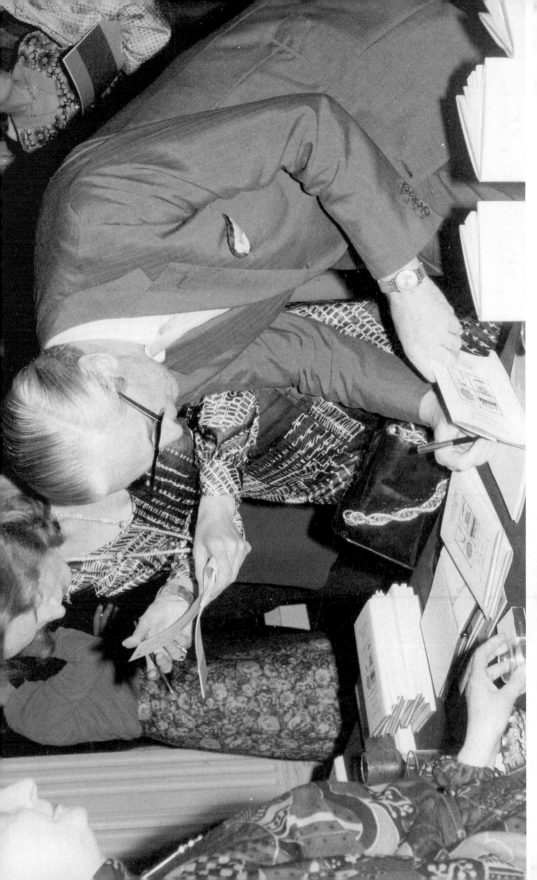

11. Conducting Seaford Silver Band, 1981.

12. Master's degree, Keele University, 1982.

13. Newick Church 'team', 1988.

14. An elephant ride in India with Betty in 1990.

15. Deputizing for Dame Vera Lynn at the RAF Regiment Memorial in Plumpton, 2000.

16. Thanksgiving service at Sussex County Cricket Club for former England captain, David Sheppard, 2005.

thought I would be prone to establish my presence in this way but, needless to say, I kept quiet. How I managed to hear of it, I do not know but, apparently, the Group Captain said to his two staff Squadron Leaders (no doubt both eager for promotion) 'I don't think Wing Commander Manwaring would fit in here, do you?' They quite agreed, naturally!

By that time, the advance through Burma was going particularly well. Senior officers were, some of them anyway, falling by the wayside (health and release) and I was appointed to command or head up all the Regiment Units in Burma from a position in Rangoon, soon to be nominated as RAF Burma, HQ.

Incidentally, I would describe Jack Harris, who eventually became Commandant-General of the Regiment from 1959 until 1961, as a man of very considerable administrative skills who, I believe, had received training as a staff officer. He was not exactly warm or particularly likeable but seemed very able. When the Regiment was founded in 1942, the first commandant, from 1942 until 1945, was Major General Sir Claude Liardet and he was succeeded by Major General A. E. Robinson to occupy the position for three years. Liardet came out of the Territorial Army tradition but Robinson was an infantryman. After those two early appointments, which undoubtedly gave the Regiment high standards of discipline and efficiency, subsequent chiefs of the Regiment came from the RAF, thus demonstrating the fact that the Corps was by then very much part of it.

Group Captain Kingsley Oliver in a superb book, *The RAF Regiment at War 1942-1946* (Leo Cooper, 2002) traces the birth, growth and evolution of the Regiment from its beginnings in the UK to immediate involvement in North Africa and the Middle East; then two years in

Europe and the same period in south-east Asia. Kingsley Oliver went through Sandhurst and served the Regiment with distinction in many capacities.

In this book, the role of the Regiment in different theatres of war is set out in commendable details and helps me to remember the different airfields which we were called upon to occupy as the war against Japan progressed. Lord Louis Mountbatten was in supreme command from his remote headquarters in Kandy and very occasionally he was to be seen near the front line. I was introduced to him at last and when he asked me how long I had been in Burma I told him it was one year, to which he countered, 'Oh quite a new boy'. After the long haul down the central plain, I definitely felt much more than a new boy!

On another occasion, the war being as good as over, I was asked to assemble as many Regiment personnel as possible for a pep talk. Mountbatten began by telling us, 'Last night I was dining with General McArthur in Okinawa'. Dining was not exactly the experience of war-weary personnel – at least not one with which they could empathize and I remember thinking at the time, 'Surely there are better ways of getting on terms with us'. Lord Louis, I judge, was a man of commanding presence who owed quite a lot to his being the son of Prince Louis of Battenberg (1854-1921). He had entered the Navy as a boy in 1913 and did two years as supreme Allied Commander in south-east Asia before becoming Viceroy of India in 1947 and then, for two terrible years, Governor General of India. Victim of an IRA bomb, his very distinguished career was brought to an untimely conclusion in 1979. Personally, I think Lord Louis was one the last achievers to be born with several silver spoons in his mouth.

It is interesting to note, from Kingsley Oliver's book, how many different Regiment squadrons passed through the new airfields, (courtesy of the Sappers), which were hurriedly built in the general advance. My own unit, No. 2743 was at Sinthe, Ondaw and Ondauk and in its capacity as a field unit occupied a new strip each time. We escaped the Battle of Meiktila and, at the end of the war, reached Mingaladon, Rangoon's airport. Several squadrons were equipped as light anti-aircraft units and there were three Armoured Car Squadrons formed at Secunderabad in February 1945.

Understandably, the Regiment is proud of creating a fighting force to occupy and defend airfields, thus relieving the Army of that responsibility. In the process the Regiment became battle-hardened and was increasingly able to take on new roles as warfare changed its character.

When I reported for duty in Rangoon to the Air Marshal Commanding he told me that I was the sort of person he would be putting forward for an honour, adding, 'If you stay long enough'. Sadly, I do not think I did but, in any event, the gong never materialized. Boy Boucher, as he was called by some, was short of stature and it was said that he wore high heels, higher than usual anyway!

Rangoon was always the destination for the victorious forces, some having come down the Imphal plain and others, myself included, through central Burma, via Mandalay. Bill Slim, General most popular, commanded the XIVth Army in the advance and I often had the honour of attending local army briefing sessions giving us a picture of the overall military situation. However, in the very early days of the war in south-east Asia, before the establishment of the Regiment, ground gunners, of which I was once one in the UK, were there but in a rather disorganized style. Bill Slim's army was often referred to as the Forgotten Army, at least until the war in Europe was over in May 1945. We celebrated VE day as best we could in central Burma but the local Japs decided to join in the war and pelted us with their grenades, thinking that our very light celebrations were worthy of their own contribution.

I often reflect on the way we spent our evenings in Burma and I recall how, nostalgically, we would sit around in semi-darkness recalling the different restaurants in the UK, which we had known. Also, we would sing our own light-hearted songs of which I remember *Fifty thousand Pongos on the Imphah Plain* (Pongo being our affectionate name for the Army) and *My Father Knew Bill Slim, Bill Slim knew my father*, a variant of which was *Lloyds Bank knew my father, my father knew Lloyds Bank*. Someone introduced us to a clever way of making our own drinking glasses and this was by means of filling an empty beer bottle with boiling oil and sharply tapping off the top to produce a remarkably clean break. The monsoon broke in May 1945 and such was the feeling of relief that one felt refreshed by standing out, semi-naked, in the rain.

In Burma, dacoits (local revolutionary elements, on a very disorganized basis) had often to be persuaded, as we went about our main duties, to lay down their arms but on one occasion the officer, sleeping in the next bed to me, was stabbed in the back as he slept under his mosquito net. Fortunately, it was not fatal.

No. 224 Group of the RAF was the constitutional name of the RAF combat unit which came down the Arakan, the coastal area of Burma and No. 221 group that which occupied the central plain both reaching Rangoon.

Together they became HQ Burma. Kingsley Oliver so rightly mentions the frequent movement of squadrons operationally in Burma. It was a taxing business but always encouraging to be going in the right direction. I see from my diary that we were in defence at Onbauk on 11 March and on 14 March in a similar position at Ondau.

One of my lasting memories of Burma concerns a most exemplary chaplain by the name of Gerald Gregson. Although it was quite impossible for the chaplains to cover all the units deployed in the campaign, Gerald did a magnificent job in holding together, as Chaplain in Chief South-East Asia, the few in chaplaincy service available. He was designated Wing Commander in rank but never wore more than the insignia of a Squadron Leader, in an effort to give his fellow chaplains a feeling of equality. He was known to give up his bed, when required, to any visiting officer and having met me in Rangoon just before he went home on leave, he made a point of telephoning my wife to assure her I was well. After the war I visited him when he became vicar of Leamington Spa, Warwickshire – a great Christian.

Whenever possible, we staged inter Squadron football matches but otherwise there was little light relief from vigilance and movements.

At Onbauk it seems from a diary entry that we were accompanied by 2495 Squadron under Squadron Leader Garnett (who later became headmaster of Marlborough), 2968 Squadron under Squadron Leader Dutton and 2960 Squadron under Squadron Leader Clarke, all of whom, I am sorry to say, I have by now almost completely forgotten. Personnel moved in and out of positions with their units with remarkable frequency.

I was fortunate enough at some stage, not, of course

while we were on the move southwards, to go on a few days leave to Nepal. It must, I think, have been after we reached Rangoon and I went with a friend to Kalimpong, a high spot in a largely unknown country. We were guests at a school run by a gentleman called Duncan and much enjoyed vistas of the Himalayas and a few quiet days away from the monsoon. However, after only a few days a signal arrived telling me to return at once for we were all on the move for Singapore. Having reached Nepal from Calcutta in a small slow train I, leaving my friend behind, went on my way, an all too brief leave ended.

About this time I changed Adjutants, John Buckman, always the most entertaining of companions, who had spooked a couple of young ladies for the whole of an evening meal that he was, in fact, none other than Groucho Marx, went off to the depot at Secunderabad to a similar posting when one by the name of Parlett came to take his place. Release groups were also making changes necessary and comings and goings, for one reason or another, were always part and parcel of daily routine. Furthermore 'resettlement' was in the air and lectures in Rangoon were becoming obligatory for us. I was a member of a court martial responsible for charging two corporals with demanding money with menaces from an elderly Chinese restaurateur called Law Po Chye – all part of my extra mural duties in the more settled atmosphere of Rangoon. Five years on from the Battle of Britain we had time to celebrate that notable victory with a service in the cathedral.

The Japanese as prisoners were, en bloc, an encouraging sight as I remember seeing 200 or 300 of them, all short of stature and huddled together awaiting the next move. They always seemed very docile in that condition although were known to be fierce in combat. We were issued with kukri knives, as used by the Gurkhas and handy for hacking your way through undergrowth. We lost one officer, not in enemy involvement but when he was shot dead accidentally (or was it on purpose?) as he was returning to camp late one night and, when challenged by the guard, failed to stop. He was young and, as we learned later, unpopular. I found writing the letter to his parents nearly impossible.

When we reached Mingaladon, Rangoon's nearest airfield, the excitement signalling the end of the campaign was, quite naturally, most palpable. From both routes, the army and the air force, in many units and formations, finished up round about VJ Day in August and one of the most exhilarating occasions, for me anyway, was when 200 or 300 service personnel decided to hold a *Songs of Praise* gathering in one of the large assembly points in Rangoon. They asked me to lead the occasion and someone, as I recall, sang a most appropriate solo:

> Be still, my soul, thy God doth undertake
> To guide the future as he hath the past.

Round about the time of this *Songs of Praise* I recall that, with Gerald Gregson, we visited the Bishop of Rangoon and squatted on the floor with local Christians remembering life during the war.

Rangoon, later in 1945 became a focal point for some of the formalities of the Japanese defeat and the climax came when a delegation arrived at the airfield headed by Lieutenant General Numata in a green Dakota aircraft painted with a white cross for ease of identification. I was appointed officer in charge of the proceedings and Air Vice Marshal Boucher led the official receiving of

Generals surrendering their precious swords in token of surrender. Everything went according to plan and the Japs left in quick time, their duty done. It was for me a defining moment.

After considerable feelings of relief that the war was over, we were then ordered to drive south through Malaya, via Kuala Lumpur with a brief trip to Penang. I travelled in my Jeep and the objective was to collect ourselves together as squadrons ready to advance on Java and Sumatra, which were far from being in a settled political state. The pre war role of the Dutch was not by then acceptable and so we knew that there were going to be problems. Before leaving Rangoon we had the very pleasurable duty of welcoming back into freedom many who had been prisoners of war in Indo-China and Siam where they had endured the most dreadful conditions. Part of the process was to give them a real welcome back into normality but for some the shock was more than they could take all at once so they pleaded with us not to send them home to Europe immediately but allow them some time to get their breath back.

In Singapore there were more celebrations and victory parades but there I received the news that my Release Group had come up and I was entitled to go home immediately. I was offered my war substantive rank of Wing Commander if I chose to stay on but the pull of wife and family was much too great and I headed back to Bombay as fast as I could to wait in the Transit Camp for a voyage home.

The thought of going further in south-east Asia had little appeal – Dutch colonial rule in the East Indies was now outdated and the Australian Wing Commander who took my place was promptly thrown into jail by a people who classified all white people as hostile. Once again I had missed out on a very unpleasant and perhaps dangerous episode and felt very thankful to be on board that famous ship, the *Queen Mary*, press-ganged into use as a troop carrier to see us home. It squeezed through the Suez Canal.

On the *Queen Mary* I shared a moderately luxurious cabin with a fellow Wing Commander by the name of Kenneth Slingsby-Farne who had been in the Far East for too long as head of catering somewhere or other and was generally reckoned by some on board who knew him to be a bit round the bend. I think we got on well together, doubtless both elated at the prospect of heading back for England, really none the worse for wear. Kenneth's special delight was to stop a young officer walking round the deck and ask him if he would like to send a message home. 'Yes, of course', was the innocent unsuspecting reply whereupon the recipient of the invitation was brought down to our cabin for the treatment. Kenneth slipped into the loo, came out with a toilet roll and invited Flight Lieutenant X or Y to write a message home on one end of the roll. That done, the prankster went back into the loo, pressed the button and, returning, triumphantly announced, somewhere in the Med, 'It will be there in five minutes'.

Kenneth had told me that he owned a half share in a very up-market restaurant in Jermyn Street, St James's, by the name of *à L'Ecu de France* but when, a civilian again, I called there a few months later enquiring after my cabin mate, no one had ever heard of him – another of his hallucinations!

A Memory of VJ Day, Rangoon

Law Po Chye, the restaurateur,
Stood in the Court House until noon;
Under his walnut skin there burned
A spirit dimmed by the long monsoon.

Corporal Snooks and Corporal Snod,
Charged with menacing old Po Chye,
Bursting with indignation stand,
While the time of the white man passes by.

Randle Manwaring

Premonition in Burma

We heard you sing the songs of France
In the mess at midnight,
While the parched earth bathed her burning face
Under the starlight.

The tent was filled with memories
As your fingers strayed
Over the strings of the guitar,
So easily you played.

Next day we stood beside your grave
Carved in the mountain side,
Remembering the liberty
For which you died.

The trumpet sounded and the fire
Of rifles smote the air.
(How fearlessly a man last night
Of death became aware).

Randle Manwaring

Thoughts from Rangoon
August, 1945

I was away last spring
On the torrid plains
Of Mandalay:
I saw the city burn and fall
Under the stars
And watched the slow unhurried trail
Of creaking carts
Beyond Shwebo,
Patiently, in the cruel heat
Returning home.
Still there was colour, strength and song
In the Burmese heart
And a concert given
By their loyal troops and dancing girls
In the cool of night
On the arid waste
At Ondaw. Then the strip was quiet
And free from ops.
That was in March;
No blossom and no English green
Was there; no Devon lane
All primroses or wood
Thick with violets soft and dark
On Surrey hills.
Now people talk
Of going East to Bangkok and Saigon -
Chinese Cafés
And less rain.
But give me back before next Spring

64

My English soil,
When new life's afoot
At Massingham and Marlborough,
After the wind
Gentle and warm,
Clears the snow from the roads at home.

Randle Manwaring

Chapter 4

Shadows of War

When I joined the Clerical, Medical and General Life Assurance Society in 1929, at the start of the great Economic Depression, the Head Office staff numbered about fifty and at the branches, say Glasgow, Birmingham, Manchester etc., not forgetting the senior London offices in the City and West End, there were roughly another twenty. By the outbreak of war in 1939, gentle growth in the business had raised the 15 St James's Square staff number a little.

The war years 1939–1945 threw up a challenging and interesting problem for the management of the Society, in that a total of sixty-two male staff members went into the armed forces and, on demobilization, came back into service. Also, three or four young men had perished in the war and during that time a member of the management took on the responsibility of keeping in touch with all those absent in the Forces. His name was Bernard Smither, officially at that time, I think, the Secretary and there is absolutely no doubt that he was ideally suited for the task. He had come up through the ranks at the Clerical, without technical qualifications but he was a charming, able gentleman who wrote to us all regularly and undoubtedly greatly helped us to remain loyal to our peacetime employer.

Being away in the Forces, possibly abroad, probably represented, for those remaining at home, problems of understanding life in the war situation but the Society initially put all on active service on half pay and, as I was earning the princely annual salary of £300, I received £150 in monthly instalments. Quite what was the rationale I am not sure but circa 1943, the Society decided, for officers anyway, to reduce the allowance to, I think, one third of 1939 salary, for me to £100 per annum. This infuriated me, so I wrote a letter to the management along the lines, 'Did they realize what it is like fighting in North Africa or Burma?' The reply came swiftly, not from Bernard Smither but from Andrew Rowell, by then General Manager and Actuary, reminding me that there were plenty of young men like me who would have counted it a privilege to work for the Society, etc. etc. So I was duly put in my place and it was arranged that on my next leave I was to go to No. 15 St James's Square to meet the Chief Executive. This I did (in my uniform of a Squadron Leader, as I was by then) and for good measure my wife Betty and Rosemary, then aged eighteen months came, waiting in the main office while I was being interviewed. Sir Andrew Rowell, as he became, was the most able and pleasant of men which probably accounts for the fact that I do not recall a single feature of the meeting, which passed off very happily, as if nothing had happened.

Another interesting piece of conversation came down to me somehow indicating the awful problem of ex-servicemen adjusting to a return to office life, when J. B. Williams, always regarded as the epitome of Clerical

Medical loyalty and also that of a Territorial Army Officer, was talking with Sir Andrew on the former's return to No. 15 and JB, explaining how fortunate he was in Army life (then a major) in being able to 'phone for a driver who would immediately come and take him anywhere'. The Chief Executive, who had an often malicious but always acute sense of humour replied, remembering his brief time in First World War service, before becoming an actuary, 'Well, JB, I was in a similar position but I was the driver!'

It is, I think, of considerable interest to analyse the staff of the Society in the Forces and how they fared during the six years plus, they spent before returning to full time service with their peacetime employers. The following analysis derives from the reverse of a menu for a Complimentary Dinner which was given by members of the staff, who served in HM Forces 1939-1945, to Mr Bernard Smither at the Trocadero Restaurant on 15 November 1946.

	Officers	Other Ranks	Total
Royal Navy	4	-	4
Royal Marines	2	-	2
Army	36	5	41
Royal Air Force	7	8	15
	49	13	62

It would be possible to draw several facts, trends and even conclusions from these figures. First of importance is the fact that several of those who served in the Army pre-war, were already in Territorial Units and became half colonels post-war. They had distinguished careers as soldiers pre-war, in the war and post-war. The five who remained in the ranks of the Army included one who, in due course, went on to reach the board of the Society, so there can be no logical general conclusion between service rank attained and success post-war. One might pose a couple of interesting but rather flippant extra questions concerning those who, like me, served in the RAF. One is that six of those seven officers were demobilized as flight lieutenants but there were over twelve Army officers with the rank of major (one rank higher), so was promotion easier in the Army? Of course not! An even more whimsical point might be made concerning the eight who, for one reason or another, remained in the ranks in the RAF. Was life, as they knew it, so comfortable that a commission seemed hardly worth it?

Needless to say, there were those who, officially designated as ex-service, only returned to the Society for a short while, seeking and finding pastures new. Only a few turned their backs on the Society; it cannot have been easy, in post-war recovery time, to find a brand new career but some did.

I certainly found it very easy to turn my back on my wartime experiences and I suppose the chief reason was that I had a wife and two children waiting for me in the UK. Rosemary was now going on four and David, only one, when I came home. The other reason is, I suppose, fascinating or impossible to evaluate but I must give some examples to make my point. After the celebration of VJ Day in Rangoon there was a parade of RAF officers addressed by Lieutenant General Messervy at which we were all given, symbolically, Japanese swords and, although I accepted mine with good grace, I quickly and without any difficulty, disposed of it. Coming through the Arabian Sea on my way home and as soon as I decently could, after leaving Bombay, I threw my personal revolver overboard. I certainly wasn't a pacifist but something within me was, I suppose, or was I very keen to get on with the next move? The final clue to my change of heart was that at the Bernard Smither dinner, quite rightly, almost everyone wore their regimental tie but I didn't wear either my RAF or my RAFVR tie but instead something rather casually non-service in style.

I suffered from phlebitis immediately after my return to the UK and this was, in all probability due to the heat in Burma and the fact that I wore a protective kind of spat round my ankles. I was confined to bed for about a week in our house in Cheam which I rented during the war as a home for my widowed mother. She generously moved out into a rented situation not far away in West Ewell where some friends of hers did her a kindness. So, for the first time, Betty, Rosemary, David and I set up home together – three up and three down – close to the shops and the station. Turning out to become one of life's coincidences, a close friend of mine, Hugh Ratcliffe, in January 1946, just demobilized from the Army brought to meet me his fiancée, Mary Blackburn. The four of us, many years later, went on holiday together to Switzerland, and even later, in fact in 2002, Mary, by then a widow and I a widower married, the new couple having known each other for about fifty-six years!

I would now like to go back to the problems which employers and employees faced as men and women returned to work post-war and, rather naturally, I am calling on my knowledge of the Clerical Medical and General Life Assurance Society where I clocked up ten years service by the time I left them, temporarily, in 1939. At that stage, I was number two in a three man

71

Underwriting Department with only one senior and one junior to me (both were in the Territorials pre-war). The work was, compared with that in other departments, interesting and easy, with pressure only occasionally. At only £300 a year in pay it was hardly surprising that this was raised to about £800 when, in 1946 over six years later, I returned to No. 15. So, to try and imagine the feelings of the sixty-two men who went off to the Services in 1939, I think it would be fair to say that we were glad to have had the opportunity of doing our bit for our country, leaving our safe jobs on ice and wondering quite what would happen to us in the war years.

As a group we were reasonably well-educated, nearly all from public schools, and as men in the Forces, prepared for almost anything. However, the men who survived the war became an entirely different breed and posed for both themselves and their employer a few difficult questions. From the employer's point of view, there were those who had remained in the Society's active employ, either at Beaconsfield or in London (here and there some still in branches) and doubtless these loyal members of staff felt that they were the ones in possession and were owed something for their trouble in bearing the burden and heat of the day, such as it was, including bombs, blitz, doodlebugs and flying bombs, if any.

Then there were the returning staff, forty-nine of whom had become officers in the services and the men and women who had remained at home might perhaps have said, or thought of us 'Who do they think they are?' As far as we were concerned, I am sure we fully appreciated the static nature of the business in wartime and frankly there were not the attractive jobs to offer us except perhaps to the Outdoor Staff, the branch mangers for instance who, generally, could conveniently slip back into

72

an office in Glasgow or wherever, as before.

If I may particularize by using my own predicament, I mention the fact that in 1945, with the rank of wing commander, I was responsible, in Burma, for about twenty RAF Regiment Squadrons, each with a compliment of 200 – 300 officers and men scattered over a wide area. Circumstances played a big part in my being promoted and positioned in that way. I therefore fully appreciate the fact that, with the best will in the world, the management of the Clerical Medical in 1946 could not possibly offer me any position remotely comparable in responsibility with that in Rangoon.

So, when I reported to No. 15 St James's Square in late January 1946, I was informed that I was to work in the Circularization Department. Now, if I had been asked at that time to nominate the most deadly dull, awful department to work in, I would quickly have quoted the one to which I was being assigned. When I reported to my new boss (again I was to be number two out of three), stuttering rather badly, poor chap, he said, 'Sit down Manwaring' – always surnames in those days – 'the war turned you from a clerk into a Wing Commander; my job is to turn you from a Wing Commander into a clerk, see?' I certainly did see and my junior was the very man, who, almost seven years earlier, had been my junior in the Underwriting Department. It was not a propitious start to my post-war career - anything but! Furthermore, prospects were, at the time, quite unknown, for it was too early to offer some kind of career path to any of us.

Meanwhile, there was good fortune on the home front. The house in which we were living in Cheam was offered to me as a sitting tenant for £3,750, so I was able to buy on very favourable terms but I cannot remember how I managed to muster the required capital. I do recall that

I did not need a mortgage.

By the way, I would like to mention that quite a lot of good natured bantering took place between ex-service personnel returning to the Clerical and those who had remained in its service 1939–1946, mainly working in the Beaconsfield office to which, not unnaturally, a few local ladies had, in the course of the evacuation, been recruited for clerical/secretarial work and a number of these were quite 'county' in style. The Beaconsfield Bucks contingent was sometimes referred to by their ex-service colleagues as 'the Royal Beaconsfield Regiment' and at one convivial tea-party in late January 1946, I remember J. B. Williams, leader of the returning men, being quizzed by two of the charming ex-Beaconsfield ladies about a demobilized Army captain who was, admittedly, a bit wet. 'I thought you said that the cream of the Society's staff were in the Forces, JB', said one very attractive and perhaps hopeful twenty-something. 'Yes, I did', replied JB (ex major) 'but this one is part of the clotted cream'. *Nil desperandum*, I remember that one of the Beaconsfield ladies did, in fact, invite my junior colleague out to lunch and very soon married him. The clotted cream must have had its attractions!

The clouds of the Second World War hung over the United Kingdom but like everything in human experience, they soon disappeared as things generally got better. However, one of the long-running war factors influencing post-war society was the menace of the U-Boat (*Unterseeboot* or undersea boat) perfected in its deadly use by the Germans in the Second World War. These cleverly used craft sank millions of tons of shipping, mainly in convoy from the USA to the UK or to the Soviet Union. This same kind of craft was also skilfully used by the USA against the Japanese and resulted in Japanese merchant shipping (276 war vessels) being sunk. This worldwide disturbance of normal trade meant that rationing of food and clothing became a feature of life continuing but, in due course forgotten, in the immediate post-war years.

In an excellent book published by Ebury Press in 1994, entitled *The Best Butter in the World*, Bridget Williams, archivist of Sainsbury's, gives most interesting details of rationing and, incidentally, many of us would be surprised to learn that self-service shopping, viewed suspiciously by many, at the time, was only introduced to the shops about the same time as rationing and, before that, we all dealt with separate counters for butter, ham, sugar etc. What a pleasant experience that was!

Local food offices were set up pre-war to deal with rationing in Britain. This meant the issue of individual ration books – a huge task. In November 1939, everyone was advised to register with a retailer of their choice and so the stage was set. Butter, bacon and sugar were the first goods to be rationed in 1940, then margarine and cooking fats, with cheese joining in by July 1940. Later, jam and similar items became rationed and all this involved the use of ration books. Everyone had to re-register twice a year. (We British were always the most long suffering of people.) To add to the complications of vital food rationing, goods in short supply, like sausages, meat pies and custard, were sold on a points basis, which was extended over many other grocery items later in 1941.

VE day and VJ day brought enormous relief to a world torn apart by the Second World War but, put in real terms, Britain had then to pay for a war, bringing it to the verge of bankruptcy. Lend-Lease, that generous agreement with the United States, enabling us to buy essential supplies on credit, had come to an end in August 1945 and obtaining what we needed became most stringent in terms since, understandably, attention would now be focussed on the needs of the liberated European countries which had been devastated by war.

The situation in Britain was highlighted by the fact that in May 1945 rations of cooking fat and meat were reduced and, unbelievably, as we might think nowadays, bread and potatoes, neither restricted in wartime, both became subject to some sort of control. Food imports had to be reduced and everyone had temporarily to face buying less than pre-war.

But clouds began to lift and in December 1948, jams and preserves became the first items to be de-rationed and, celebrating the event, one Sainsbury manager set his staff the goal of selling 10,000 pounds of jam in the first week of deregulation. So it went on – milk was controlled until January 1950 but remained on a points system for a further four months. Tea came off in October 1952, sweets in February, eggs in March 1953 and not until well into 1954 did butter, margarine and cheese come off rationing. Finally, in July 1954 bacon and meat drew the curtain down on wartime rationing!

Meanwhile, the big, wide world was not really at peace and Betty and I, with our three children (Michael was born in 1946) – with thousands of other families – had to clothe and feed our families as best we could; like everyone else, we managed. I had taken up my duties at the Clerical but was quickly moved to run the office of the West End branch. It gave me the experience of servicing the outdoor staff there, of working under a delightful manager, Douglas Gordon MacKay and gaining a taste of the production side by being in contact with some of the main sources of new business in the

West End; Lloyds Bank, Cox's and King's branch, Pall Mall, Gieves in Old Bond Street, also bankers Glyn Mills and Grindlays, which all ran flourishing insurance advisory services for their customers. This appointment was definitely a move forward in my career in the insurance industry. It gave me real contact with the products and the producers.

One of the most threatening clouds to hang over us in the post-war years was undoubtedly that of communism, mainly represented by hostility between the USA and the Soviet Union. The term Cold War was coined in 1947 by Bernard Baruch (1870-1965), economist and close adviser to three American Presidents and the words encapsulated a fear of a nuclear war, as everyone realized the ghastly horrors of Hiroshima and Nagasaki. The Cold War was therefore fought on ideological, economic and political fronts, and the term Iron Curtain came into use.

The 1950s represented the bitter conflict between the ideologies of East and West but détente was eventually achieved by the 1970s and virtual control of atomic energy production was managed by a United Nations Commission.

In 1948, moving to a larger property in Cheam we were able to house our three children very comfortably and at the same time, actually from my return from the RAF in 1946, I was able to throw myself into the work of Sutton Crusaders, which in wartime and despite shortage of leaders, flying bombs etc., had been very ably managed by my old friend Douglas Kahn. Attendance at the Sunday afternoon meeting in Christian discipleship was 100 – 150, boys only and, when compared with the well-scripted problems in the early twenty-first century of Sunday Schools etc., indicates the great changes in the climate of work among teenagers which has occurred.

At the annual camps organized by Crusader Headquarters, Sutton in one year I remember, sent 100 officers and boys. The work of leadership involved commitment but was very rewarding. Cricket and rugby matches at Epsom College were highlights, and there were exciting annual national sporting events in athletics and seven-a-side rugby, in both of which Sutton often came out on top.

In 1940, just before I was sent into the RAF, I had been instrumental in starting a follow-up to Crusaders in the Sutton Area, which eventually took on the name of Wellesley. Membership was open to boys and girls of fifteen and over and it was supported by Crusader units in Banstead, Carshalton Beeches, Cheam, Epsom, Ewell and Sutton. Many have since described the Wellesley Fellowship as unique. It had, at its peak, a membership of nearly 200, tennis was available at our home each week in the summer, a mixed hockey team played against teams from All Souls, Langham Place and large suburban churches and, above all, there was a monthly gathering in Sutton to which nationally known speakers came. Between sixty and seventy years after its inauguration and several decades after it folded, I, for one, can see the overall benefits of the Wellesley and I have for long thought it was the best thing which, in starting by the grace of God, I achieved. Long term and widely different benefits continue to be recognized.

Incidentally, but not inconsequently, during my period of Sutton Crusader leadership, I had the satisfaction of seeing nearly twenty young men enter the ordained ministry of the churches, just over half being Anglicans.

War clouds in 1950 centred on Korea and British Forces were involved. It may be remembered that the north versus south war, between communist and non-communist forces, occupied the years 1950-1953 and finished indecisively. General Douglas Macarthur (1880-1964), an outstanding USA strategist, commanded the UN forces in Korea, whilst China sided with the opposition in the north. Five million people died in the Korean War – another terrible waste.

In 1951, I managed to get my first slim volume of poetry published by The Fortune Press. For me this proved to be a defining and extraordinary experience. I was thirty-nine years of age and had been writing verses for possibly twenty years but had had little success in getting items into poetry magazines and, realizing that unless an aspiring poet had been recognized in magazine terms, there was, speaking generally, little chance of a publisher offering to do a slim volume. However, one R. A. Caton, who owned and ran this small publishing house, agreed to bring out my work and I found myself in excellent poetic company or so it turned out. On his list were many who became recognized (or had already been recognized) for their ability, including Kingsley Amis, Thom Gunn, Martin Seymour-Smith, Cecil Day-Lewis (who became Poet Laureate), Roy Fuller, Wilfred Gibson, Lord Alfred Douglas, Philip Larkin (whom many thought ought to have become Poet Laureate) and Dylan Thomas. Mr Caton published an amazing total of 600 books, mostly poetry, and died in 1971, aged seventy-four. In R A Caton and the Fortune Press (Bertram Rota, 1983) Timothy d'Arch Smith collected details of this man and his work and records the fact that Cecil Day-Lewis found Caton to be a slum landlord in Brighton and Larkin referred to him as a lazy sod. Caton founded The Fortune Press in 1924 and had an office near Victoria Station in London where he did all the work, including packing. He also had ninety-one properties in Brighton, with little sanitation. He loved discarded newspapers and made several journeys to London every day collecting his wares. He used printers all over the country and I recall that, in my presence, he remonstrated with one firm about the non-delivery of my books. Hardly surprising, he never paid any royalties and one day he arrived at No. 15 St James's Square with a box of my unsold books declaring, 'These are instead of royalties'. He left over £129,000 to St Margaret's Church, Rottingdean.

In 1948, at the Clerical Medical, I was appointed a departmental head, responsible for branch liaison and keeping records of the Society's agents. Additionally I was editor of *Clerical Notes*, then a duplicated quarterly on staff affairs. E. F. Phillips, a member of the management, was also appointed to oversee, and my friend, Graham Ward, with whom I often played squash, provided details of 'hatches, matches and despatches'.

At about that time I became an assistant editor of a poetry magazine called *Envoi* and a few years later, for five years, I took on the editorship of the *Crusader* quarterly – a demanding assignment. So I kept my hand in with the literary world (of a kind)!

Undoubtedly, I owed a great deal, in terms of my huge interest in poetry, to the encouragement of Walter de la Mare, whom my father had helped through his work at the London Library, in producing material for de la Mare's books. This great poet had been very compli-mentary over the publication of my first slim volume in 1951 and I sent him a poem, which he acknowledged, registering his eightieth birthday in 1953. He sympa-thized with me over the many rejections I had had from editors of poetry magazines and told me that he had received enough rejections to '...paper my bedroom'.

However, later I had the extremely good fortune of my poems being used on both BBC and ITV programmes – on the former in one item used to illustrate descriptive verse and on the latter in a week's epilogue kind of series. I appeared in numerous anthologies, a school assembly collection and, wonder of wonders in 1957, a Japanese professor included one of my poems in his collection *How to read an English Poem.* The book, in particular, included poems by famous English poets and was produced, giving for each poem, the two languages appearing on opposite pages.

On a holiday in the USA I visited the log cabin, in Vermont, where Robert Frost wrote much of his poetry and was invited to meet some of the staff at Middlebury College, where he lectured, and where I was introduced by a vice president as being akin to their Wallace Stevens, '...an Insurance Executive by vocation and a poet by avocation' (hyperbole).

Attending a party in Bermuda at a later date, where I met many Americans, I asked them, innocently I think, what they thought of President Nixon and Watergate and, epitomizing the rivalry felt with the Kennedy clan, partly through the then recent drowning of Mary Jo Kopechne, someone made a remarkably succinct comment saying, 'Remember, no one was drowned at Watergate'.

Shadows of war continued to darken international affairs in the 1950s particularly when President Nasser (1918-1970) of Egypt nationalized the Suez Canal; his policies as unofficial leader of the Arab world bringing him into conflict with the West. British troops were withdrawn after threatening an attack on Egypt. But more significant and damaging to international peace, actual war was started in Vietnam in 1954 and once again the United States decided to halt the spread of communism, this time in south-east Asia, and a totally wasteful war which lasted for twenty-one years, was fought between the communists in the north and the south, until the two areas were eventually joined. In the end, the US, having lost more than 50,000 troops (also, 40,000 South Vietnamese lost their lives) negotiated a peace but the Americans have never forgotten the ghastly spectre of Vietnam, where they entered the fray in 1961 and which gave rise to much domestic opposition.

I have always had an affectionate but loose relationship with the British United Provident Association (BUPA) originating from the fact that it was founded jointly, I believe, by Lord Nuffield and Sir Andrew Rowell, the latter being my chief at the Clerical, post-war. Additionally, I was friendly at No. 15 with Eric Roberts (we both hoped for promotion there but it never really came). His father knew Sir Andrew and eventually the latter invited Eric to become, in due course, Chief Executive of BUPA. From then on, Eric and I became firm friends in a business relationship; I canvassed the work of BUPA among my city friends and he invited me to become a full member (a £1 share and little responsibility) and said to me, rather unwisely I suppose, 'From among our Full Members we appoint Governors'. However, in 1966, at Eric's behest, I spent a weekend in Manchester in the course of which I appeared, pro BUPA, on an ITV programme on health care.

Sir Andrew was quite a wag and a wit and on one occasion he had a letter to which he wanted to reply, from a policyholder, who, for religious reasons, felt he had to disassociate himself from the Society and surrender his policy. Knowing that my father was next door in the London Library, Sir Andrew asked me to go there and find a suitable text that might be sent to this policyholder in reply, the gentleman having quoted from scripture. I produced from, Deuteronomy Chapter 28, verse 66, '...and shalt have none assurance of thy life'. My chief thanked me warmly.

My wonderful Aunt Helen, who financially helped the family in so many ways, and who worked in a senior position at the London Library, was described at her retirement party by Simon Nowell Smith, the Librarian, as their 'chatelaine'. She was sent the following charming letter by John Masefield, then Poet Laureate:

Dear Miss Helen,

(If this would not be too bold now, anyhow at Christmastime). I must send a few words at least of thanks for your most kind letter, and some words to wish you a most happy retirement. May your leisure be delightful to you for many years to come.

I am not sure that I shall re-visit the Library, but if I do, it will be a shock not to see you on the left as I go in, where your kindness of welcome has always (and so often) gladdened my day; and my wife's day too.

The poet Laureate had a very felicitous habit of sending out personal Christmas Cards containing a short new poem. He wrote on one such card:

For Helen Manwaring

It's Christmas Eve, and dogs do bark,
It snows, and the wind shifts;
The frost will strike the Downland stark;

Put lamp in window as a mark
For Kings come bringing gifts.

With all best wishes for now and later
from John and Constance Masefield.

Poetry, my alter ego, continued to flourish through all the vicissitudes of my working life in the world of insurance but I never regarded myself as a successful poet, only a minor one, a fact which I highlighted in a book, I hope soon to be published entitled *The Making of a Minor Poet* and which was intended to bring together in a selected volume, all the poems I felt worth keeping in that way. I was assisted in my choices by Prebendary John Pearce, always my spiritual and poetry counsellor, also by my old friends Professor Gwilym Evans and his wife Angela with their long association with my versifying. Hardly surprising, in view of my persistent labours in the field of poetry, I had the pleasure of seeing a number of anthology appearances and once or twice I was asked to write something for a specific purpose, e.g. school assemblies. But I think one of my most satisfying extras, was appearing on London Buses with an anti-smoking poem, in due course adopted by Lord McColl of Guys Hospital, hoping to cut down smoking among the nurses.

I taught poetry for a while at Northease Manor School, near Lewes where most of the boys were dyslexic. They did me the honour of making me the president of the school cricket team. As, living a few hundred yards from the school, I occasionally conducted a morning assembly for the school, I once invited any boy with a personal problem outside the school's curriculum, to have a word me after the assembly and I was approached by the son of Frankie Vaughan, the entertainer, with the question

'Excuse me, Mr Manwaring but are you a Jew?' That was all.

I was always very interested in the work of Robert Frost, the American poet and one year on holiday at St Mawes in Cornwall, we became friendly with an American attorney, Adrian Lieby who, I learned later, was a senior partner in a New York firm, Lamb, Leboef and Lieby, with common business interests in Lloyds of London. He generously invited us to stay with him in Vermont where they had a 'little old shack'. After a few days with him in New York we had the special delight of seeing the glorious colours of Vermont in the Fall but additionally, we were taken to see Frost's log cabin.

My contacts with the United States seem to have developed in a remarkable way for later one of my books of poems was published by Palancar of the US and eventually my best publishing success was with the Mellen University Press of New York which brought out two of my books of prose, one on the history of hymnody and the other on the link between poetry and hymnody. One of my further slim volumes of poems came out from Mellen about the same time.

Autumn in the Nuclear Age

Swiftly the summer passes
On swallow's wings,
Murmuring the mass migration
Of living things.

Slowly the curtain closes
On earth's festival,
Promising other roses
While petals fall.

Soon, in the splendid evening,
As the last hope dies,
A new, undreamed creation
Through flames will rise.

Randle Manwaring

In Williamsburg, Virginia

A ripening field of tall tobacco plants
between white weather-boarded houses
kept as they were two hundred years ago
and I recall a poster of my boyhood,
proclaiming a brand of English cigarettes,
the caption – Home Again From Virginia.

I now know how it was romanticised -
the leaning of the many masted ship,
ploughing the seas in glorious days of sail.
I thought of 'home' somewhere in our West Country
–Virginia sounded well upon the ear
of one who knew his Georgian poetry of place.

Now in these fields of Williamsburg,
released from slavery and colonial rule,
where brother fought with brother, I can see
a hope for all the world's new battlefields,
as still men die for causes dearly held,
for yet Virginian peace must come to them.

Randle Manwaring

Song of High Sussex

From Chanctonbury to Ditchling on to Firle
the beacons are ablaze with summer light
and South Downs Way meandering west and east
scatters the bridle paths to left and right.

By Adur, Ouse and Cuckmere watch
where quiet waters slowly southward run,
weaving their patterned fruitfulness
in green and gold, mixed by the gentle sun.

Stretch out your arms, embrace the south
from Harting through to High and Over's height
where skylark songs of downland praise
make music for her travellers' delight.

Randle Manwaring

Chapter 5

Peace and War in the City and Elsewhere

Cyril Shaw, one of the members of the management of the Clerical and with whom I sometimes played cricket, became concerned, I believe, that my career progress in the Society had become rather stunted and arranged for me to join the growing pensions department housed across the road in No. 3 St James's Square. I think the move was anticipatory, for pensions were an expanding part of the Society's business and really there was no actual position for me to go to at No. 3. However, I shared a room with Douglas Moat who had already established himself as a first class consultant on pensions, dealing with the Society's branches, City brokers and, in due course, with clients adopting the Clerical Pension Plan. I made it my business to pick up, as quickly as I could, the considerable technicalities of pensions and eventually took upon myself visits to some of the Society's slow-to-move-on-pensions branches. After about a couple of years and still without a clearly defined position, I decided to look elsewhere for my future career and found, with the help of a solicitor friend of mine, that there were one or two Lloyds Brokers, hoping to increase their life and pensions business, one of these being C. E. Heath & Co., famous because Cuthbert Heath, its founder, had been one of the most highly respected members of that fraternity. I was on holiday in Frinton at the time but came for my interview with the chairman, Charles Gould and the managing director of the Home side, Bruce Miller, and when they said they could offer me £1,500 per annum (including bonus, I was on about £1,000 at the Clerical), I daringly replied that I had made up my mind I could not accept less than £2,000. The chairman responded 'We wouldn't argue with that Bruce, would we?' So the deal was done and on 1 October 1956, I began fifteen years of exciting work in the growing pensions industry and thanks to the kindly view which Bruce Miller and the next chairman, George Ewart Thomson, took of me, I progressed in the company structure through the various echelons of management.

The person who managed Heath's life and pensions business at the time was very unwell and that was the main reason for my appointment. Sadly but fortunately for me, he died a few months later and I was appointed manager. In those days, on leaving a pensionable position, you left behind all your pension rights and, in my case also, my contributions, slight though they were, to a separate Widow's and Orphan's Fund, so I had quite a lot of pensions ground to make up.

Leaving the serene waters of the Clerical at age forty-four produced plenty of garbled good wishes from some of my colleagues like. 'We hope you will find equally good friends in your move'. However, being a committed Christian, I knew that I could rely on divine strength and guidance and I was entirely happy at leaving the more gentlemanly atmosphere of the West End of London for the equally gentlemanly but very competitive air of the City.

I quickly made friends, not only from among the officials of the various companies with whom I was placing business but also among my opposite numbers in other firms of brokers. I joined in the meetings of fellow members of the Corporation of Insurance Brokers, initially with those of the Life Society of which, in due course, I became chairman for a statutory year in office, chairing the annual dinner in the Captain's Room at Lloyds. One thing led to another and I found myself chairing the Life Assurance committee of the corporation, which dealt with ticklish disciplinary matters etc.

The Society of Pension Consultants was founded just before I joined the staff of Heaths, individual companies in the business being eligible for membership, and an elected representative from each forming the council. I sat on this for a few years and was, before very long, invited to become president. This came as a very pleasant surprise – most of those elected were actuaries and, by popular vote, the council always chose the next president.

When I chaired the S.P.C. dinner, held at Lloyds, my speaker was Richard Crossman, at that time Harold Wilson's right-hand man in Government. Crossman was, unfortunately heckled by some members. He was told by Wilson that he was a compulsive communicator – quite a compliment. These various appointments did not, I am sure, pass unnoticed by my colleagues on other sides of the business at Heaths and, in due course, the inevitable happened – the knives came out for I represented a dangerous rival to those seeing themselves as future chairmen of the company.

Looking after life and pensions business for a firm of

brokers brings one into direct contact with the client and with directors, often including the chairman, who is naturally quite interested in his own pension. This is not so with the other sides of the business – on the fire and accident side insurance managers of the big clients are effectively your clients and, on other sides, placing the business at Lloyds from the introduction of another broker source constitutes the art of the Lloyds broker. All this is not often appreciated by those on, say the American side but I always enjoyed meeting valued overseas clients at board lunches and, also could not help noticing that my knowledge of the chairmen of some larger UK clients was used in the entertaining at board lunches. I was effectively prevented from seeking business in the USA since my colleagues responsible for that area of business imagined that my involvement would possibly jeopardize their own business. Other Lloyds Brokers would pull my leg that I did not go to the States! Ironically, I remember one of Heath's American broker clients at lunch telling me I definitely ought to visit them but, sadly, that was not allowed.

The beginning of troubles at Heaths occurred when it became evident that the net profits of the company were too low, a fact which would have come to light earlier had there been a qualified accountant in the set-up. One was appointed and, being a complete pragmatist with terra firma feelings, he managed to become *persona grata* with the chairman, a person of similar outlook, and set about bringing the finances into line. I am quite sure that meetings were planned without my knowledge, (I was then a managing director of the main board), evening get-togethers were arranged and plans were laid for formulating profitability. Concurrently, a firm of accountants, assuming quite easily the extra role of management consultants, was now given the task of producing a report on the management structure and I had been visited by a fellow MD who asked me to believe that someone would be coming to see me 'just to find out what we all do'. I innocently accepted the ploy.

At about the same time the chairman decided to have a straw vote on his successor in the chair and although, naturally, the result was never divulged, someone in the know told me that I received one vote less than the favourite. The result was hardly surprising given the fact that, on the board, there were about six directors on the American side, two on the marine and, apart from the vice chairman himself, one on the aviation, with another on home business. Each had one vote.

When the consultants produced their report, which was not passed round the board, a never-to-be-forgotten board meeting was called and the chairman announced a proposed holding company board, three or four, of which I was not one and then an operating company and again my name was omitted. The die was already cast, sufficient votes had been assured but we were invited to comment, there being three other more junior directors for the chop. I spoke: 'Well Mr Chairman, as the most senior member affected, perhaps I could say a few things'. I then enumerated some points, which I thought were in my favour – through me we had just bought very cheaply indeed, a firm of brokers in Reading complete with a property, thrown into the deal for free and eventually sold for over a million. We had just completed the biggest life assurance policy ever done in the London market and we had more pensions business enquiries in the pipe-line than ever before.

I was, however, wasting my breath for there was no voting but I wrote on my scribbling pad 'God is calling me to something new'. That board meeting finished mid-morning, just in time for me to get ready to attend the retirement lunch for Winifred Rosson who was, I think, the first woman to be appointed to a London Insurance Broker Board, in her case Heath, Urqhuart (Life and Pensions), of which I was the first managing director and to which, recognizing her skills very highly, I had appointed her a few years earlier.

At the same time I became deputy chairman of the Corporation of Insurance Brokers and was due shortly to take on the national chairmanship. Heath's chairman said he realized this in bringing forward my retirement but could do nothing about it! The market must have registered a stunned surprise. After Winifred's retirement lunch I went round to St Helen's Place in the City to attend a Corporation meeting but seeing the Secretary in the loo beforehand, he asked me how things were going and, I am afraid, I shed a few tears in answering him.

As the day dragged on after the awful board meeting, there was no real sympathy for me from my fellows and some seemed to be rubbing salt into the wound. One of the American directors volunteered the comment, 'I never thought the Life man should be on the board'. Another said 'What will you do Randle, take a local job?' I was at that time fifty-eight, going on fifty-nine so, in later times, retirement would not have been unusual but in the days of which I write, it was customary, health permitting, to retire at sixty-five, which naturally I aimed at. Fortunately I felt very fit.

There were over a 100 Heath staff given early retirement or redundancy and the cricketing comment went round the City that Heath's were 100 for 4!

To endeavour to complete the scenario of those hectic days, I must mention the company relationship with the

94

Excess Insurance Company, which had also been started by Cuthbert Heath. Its managing director was on the board of Heath but, *nil desperandum*. Excess mounted a takeover bid for Heath – whether official or unofficial I cannot remember. Not unnaturally, the matter was referred to Lloyds who ruled that it would be most improper for an insurance company to own a broking house. My own position was a little delicate since, a few years earlier, I had been instrumental in starting the Excess Life Assurance Company, which later was to suffer because of the relative troubles of the motor insurance business of Excess. Lloyds, itself at the time of the abortive takeover bid by Excess, was planning to start its own life assurance company and one of its advisers, Alec Layborn, affectionately known in the industry as 'Mr Pensions', was commissioned to find a chairman for the new Lloyds life company. Alec, whom I knew slightly, came to see me saying 'The chairman of Lloyds, Sir Henry Mance, in the knowledge that they had saved Heath from the Excess takeover threat, wonders whether Heath could release you to head up the new life company for Lloyds.' 'Alec', I quickly replied, 'Heath's have already released me, I've just been put off the Board.' In the event Jackie Mance himself decided to take on the chairmanship of the new company and wisely to appoint an actuary to manage its affairs. So, taking up the offer of a part-time desk at the Excess offices I set about conducting my small amount of affairs and, fairly soon, had offers of three different positions, it being much easier in those days to find new employment. The first offer was to become the Agency Manager of a new, but prosperous life company called Lifeguard, the second was to become deputy chairman of Anthony Gibbs, one of the smaller firms of brokers and the third, which I selected, was to join the Bank Insurance movement by becoming the Insurance Adviser of Midland Bank, with the equivalent rank, as it turned out and for what it was worth, of assistant general manager. After the intrigue, hurly burly and sadness of Heaths I guess I looked forward to walking the corridors of gentlemanly power at one of the big four banks (Midland were once the largest), and doing something quite different - in insurance.

When I look back to my time at Heaths and my eventual demise, I cannot help wondering why it was I became one of the objects of rejection by my colleagues. Like everyone else, I am sure, I had my faults but, certainly running the smallest side of the business in terms of income and profitability, I was viewed by some as having no claim to advancement.

Due to my industry appointments, which ran alongside my duties at Heath's, I naturally knew something of chairmanship, I could also make a speech and write an article. These abilities, such as they were, were held in low esteem by most of my colleagues and so, one way or another, a well disguised plan was made to make sure that I was politely (?) ousted. Some of those on the way up were fairly heavy lunchtime drinkers, often also delaying returning home in the evening for a similar reason, but fortunately, I was never invited. It was, I imagine, known that I was a regular churchgoer and, although I never had the opportunity of declaring my personal faith as a Christian, I think it was appreciated that I did my best to bring integrity into my business dealings. Some other Christians on the staff appeared grateful that I was on the board, sometimes quietly expressing as much. Two Assistant Directors at Heaths were Crusader Leaders.

In my role at Heaths I made it my business that we should always, so far as I was able, make absolute honesty the keynote of all our own dealings, for example never disguising the adverse features of a particular risk with insurance companies being approached. In later years, I had the satisfaction of being thanked by a previous member of my staff who became a barrister, for the stand which we all took. Also, I subsequently carried this tenet to my next job that everyone, within the limits of opportunities available, is entitled to be promoted to the limits of their own ability – but not beyond. Furthermore, I always held to the belief – not by any means popular in later years in big companies – that if you look after your staff, they will look after your clients and the end result will be that the shareholders, if any, will profit. Greed and materialism in the twenty-first century appear to play a dominant part.

When, in 1968 we moved as a family to Rodmell in Sussex, our three sons then unmarried and sometimes living at home, very considerable changes took place in the pattern of my life. I enjoyed the longer train journey to London, making a number of friends in so doing and we immediately started attending the village church, thereby resuming my active love for the Church of England into which I was baptised as an infant and confirmed at the age of fifteen. The village was famous for the fact that Virginia Woolf lived there for many years and committed suicide in the River Ouse which flowed not far away. I soon met a member of the village who remembered, as he put it, 'fishing her out of the river, leg-o-mutton sleeves and all'. I met quite early, in our years at Rodmell, Virginia's husband Leonard Woolf and once or twice talked with him about poetry.

With my experience behind me of teaching in

Crusaders, thereby obtaining a fair knowledge of the Scriptures, I decided to offer myself for training as a Reader in the Church of England and the Rector of Rodmell agreed so, in due course, I was assigned to the incumbent at Rotherfield who set me on my way by asking me to write a series of essays and deliver in his empty church, a specimen short sermon. He was quite a tease and would sometimes say to me things like, 'Now you know all about the Reformation, I am sure, so write 2,000 words on the Oxford Movement'. Or on another occasion 'There are, as we know, several sacraments in the church apart from baptism and marriage but I don't think I can ask you to write something on Confessions, Extreme Unction and Penance'. I don't think that I could write very much on those matters anyway, but mention of them demonstrated my tutor's Anglo-Catholic tradition - and a sense of fun!

After my licensing as a Reader I conducted services or preached on an occasional basis at both Rodmell and Southease, the nearby village with which we were united in the diocese of Chichester, the Rector writing in the parish magazine that my appointment would enable him to accept invitations to preach in other churches, something which, I remember, never happened. A year or two into my new part-time ministry, one of the church wardens in Southease asked me a searching question 'How are you getting on with our rector?' I told her that I was getting on well but her comment was very disturbing, 'You wait, my boy, your turn will come'. Within a couple of weeks my turn had come and the rector appeared not to wish for my assistance any longer. At about the same time I became friendly with the Headmaster of Northease Manor School, a short distance away and sought his consolation for my parochial rejection. He counselled, having had a similar experience in another way with the rector, 'Don't worry, at least he can't take away your readership'. As a result, the incumbent of Southover church in nearby Lewes took me under his wing and, whilst in the course of my thirty-five years stint as a Reader I think I officiated in say fifty or sixty Sussex churches, schools, nursing homes and once at the prison, I am sure I did duty at Southover more often than at anywhere else.

I suppose I am, by nature, a person who likes to get involved and, although the Rector at Rodmell made sure I was not included in deanery and diocesan affairs, I did so, in due course, in subsequent parishes, becoming elected to the deanery and diocesan synods and sought to play my part in helping to administer from a distance the complexities and frustrations of the Anglican church. The climax, if you like, of these involvements came when I was elected to serve on the bishop's council of the diocese and so began a period of fascinating experience at a theoretically decisive level in church affairs. The make-up of this body in Sussex is that for starters there are three bishops and three archdeacons and they effectively run the diocese at their own staff meetings. Then each of the three archdeaconries, Chichester, Horsham and Lewes, elects three or four clergy and three or four laymen. It is a most interesting amalgam of ability, personality, courage and fear, tradition and belief. The diocesan bishop, himself a Catholic, as was his predecessor, under whom I worked, wisely tried to preserve the different traditions of Anglicanism and so his two suffragans each represent differing Catholic and Evangelical standpoints. Further, to balance things equally, a Catholic bishop works with an Evangelical Archdeacon and the Evangelical assistant bishop has alongside him a Catholic

Archdeacon. I don't think the liberals or middle of the road churchmen get much of a look-in!

If you are one of the lay members of the bishop's council it is, in my experience, difficult to play a really active part at the meetings. I think I was the first Evangelical layman to come into the picture and I remember the then diocesan secretary, himself also a Reader, saying to me early on, 'I don't know how you are going to get on in the bishop's council'. As far as I was concerned I think I got on fairly well, just occasionally making a point, although the then chairman, the diocesan bishop, did not actually seek one's involvement. On one occasion, when the Director of Ordinands appeared before the Council to give his annual account of steward-ship and listed a high percentage of ordinands attending Catholic theological colleges I enquired, for example, about the possibility of our young men and women being assigned to say Oak Hill College in North London. The reply was wishwashy but when Wallace Benn became Bishop of Lewes I told him of this experience and he said, with a delightful twinkle, 'I think he may have to change his attitude when he realizes that I am a trustee of Oak Hill'. So the cut and thrust of bishop's council work went on but, on the whole, it is usually very positive and harmonious.

When I retired from the bishop's council, after about fifteen years in office and, taking a similar situation from the business world, I saw myself as the equivalent of a non-executive director, but all I received to mark my service was an earthenware mug. I did not think that modern bishops took much notice of a New Testament feature of that office, given to hospitality, but I would have been satisfied with a local restaurant!

One of my most rewarding experiences of the early

Sussex years was my chairmanship of the governing body of Luckley – Oakfield School in Wokingham, Berkshire, the only snag being that it was a difficult journey from where I lived. However, the school, for girls only, was half boarding and half day and progress was always being made in the building of new much needed facilities; an extra boarding house, a science block, a music centre etc. At one point we needed to sell some unwanted woodland and I wrote for some help to Margaret Thatcher who, on her way up, was then Secretary of State for Education and Science. She responded most helpfully and a few years before I had heard her speak at one of the meetings of Life Society when she was billed as a Treasury Minister, a barrister and tax counsel. On that occasion our chairman, who succeeded me in that office, ought to have invited her in the usual way, to have dinner after the meeting but, sadly, he had failed to make the arrangements beforehand, as Margaret Thatcher embarrassingly told me. My contacts with this illustrious lady did not end there and when those of us on the Life Assurance Committee of the Corporation of Insurance Brokers once found ourselves at odds with a Finance Bill, I hosted a lunch at the RAF Club on the subject and both Mrs Thatcher, then shadowing on Treasury affairs, spoke eloquently, with Peter Walker, an insurance broker MP, later to become Lord Walker, in attendance. Subsequently, the C.I.B. held a lunch time drinks party at 15 St Helen's Place and Margaret Thatcher was among our guests. As the event wore on I turned to this distinguished lady with the news that I had an invitation, for two, in my pocket from one of my clients, to attend the opening by Ted Heath, her chief then, of the Antique Dealers Fair in Chelsea Town Hall that afternoon. 'Come on' she replied, 'let's go'. Ted Heath was then Mrs

Thatcher's shadow party leader so the occasion was quite appropriate and after that I returned her by taxi to the House of Commons.

A never-to-be-forgotten week came my way in 1963, the year before I became a Director at Heaths, when, at the suggestion of an acquaintance, I gave a series of talks in the B.B.C's early morning five minutes *Lift Up Your Hearts* and travelled up from Cheam each day before going on to work. I asked my producer at one stage what was the most popular kind of programme and she quickly said 'Oh, the sort of thing, do be kind to your animals'. A slight exaggeration I expect but making a point.

As far as I can remember, the only people to comment on my broadcasts were a waitress at the RAF Club and Lionel Lee who cut my hair in the City. My fellow directors at Heath made no comment.

At Heaths my work had gone well enough for me to reach main board level and in the course of development the new chairman came to see me with the guarded information that a well-known cricketer would be placed on my staff, no name given. 'Who is to be the next England captain?', he asked. I forget the name I gave but 'No', he said, 'something like Webster'. The only cricketing Webster I knew of was W. H. Webster, deceased, playing for Middlesex years before. The conversation fizzled out but, not long afterwards, none other than Ted Dexter joined us and stayed, England tours permitting and Sussex captaincy intervening, for five or six years. When Ted went off one winter touring Pakistan with the England team, he kindly allowed his very charming (model) wife, Susan, to come as our guest to one of the Heath Christmas parties – a very popular move for us! Ted was a very popular figure with us, notable with my number two in the life and pensions business, Derek

Newton, who later became chairman, then president, of the Surrey County Cricket Club. Derek, a very able friend, also became chairman of Heaths.

Ted Dexter once invited me to have lunch with the teams at Hove, the Sussex county ground and it was for a match against Hampshire, then captained by a charismatic character, Colin Ingleby-Mackenzie. I shall not forget my horror at lunch seeing Colin sit down with us wearing a sports jacket over his white shirt. To my traditional mind, a blazer was the only proper garment to wear over whites for lunch!

My later work with Midland Bank continued apace and after a number of persuasive memos to the top management they agreed to the formation of Midland Bank Insurance Services, thus following the pattern set by Barclays with their B.I.S.CO. From then on I appointed insurance managers in all regions of the bank, from Newcastle down to Exeter and almost all came from insurance companies. For each appointment there would have been about twenty applicants so with some fifteen regions in the bank, about 300 applied, of which perhaps forty-five were short-listed. I also appointed my number two at chief office with me, plus individuals to head-up both the fire and accident and life sides of the business. I then visited each of the regions of the bank holding a day conference on insurance for managers, hoping thereby to encourage them to take up the drive for business in this field. Previously, many managers held quite lucrative personal insurance agencies, so the new system was not universally popular. Nevertheless, the work of MBIS took off; by the time I retired assistant managers had been appointed in the regions and, overall, millions of pounds profit had been registered. In due course, the big banks had to decide whether to develop as brokers on the best buy basis or go own brand, forming their separate insurance companies. One of my more expressive and very successful managers, following the bank's decision to go own brand, using a colourful picture from rugby football, said that the bank kicked the company into touch.

One of the most engaging extra mural appointments resulting from MBIS was the formation of a small committee of the bank's European partners to examine the potential of involvement in insurance marketing and I was kindly appointed chairman. We met by rotation in London, Paris, Amsterdam, Brussels, Berlin and Vienna and the agreed language for the meetings was English. However, this did not prevent the French delegate from imposing his language on our meeting in Paris where the Dutch representative came to my rescue by interpreting as necessary. At the evening dinner which followed one day's Parisian proceeding and probably to make up for my lack of French, I told a story of General de Gaulle but I realized that to tell even a small joke about the great man did not go down very well with our host who, over coffee, showed me a book presented to him by the General. I think my favourite venue for these meetings was Vienna, hosted by *Creditdanstal Bankverein*

As I was about to retire from the City, I was given the opportunity of fulfilling a long cherished ambition – to graduate. Accordingly, through the introduction of John Briggs, on the staff of Keele University, I enrolled for a three year, non-residential course for a Master's degree in history. My work was mostly done by correspondence but about every three months I visited Staffordshire and queued with the young undergraduates to see my tutor. He specialized in Victorian and modern studies and I did my thesis on the subject, which had always fascinated me, of the development of the Church of England in the twentieth century and, in particular, how the evangelicals emerged from some kind of backwater into a position of academic strength and involvement. John was himself a leading light in the Baptist church but he could not have been more helpful to me.

After that was all over and I was awarded my degree by the Chancellor, Princess Margaret, I wondered whether, with appropriate alterations, my typescript would make a sufficiently publishable proposition and quite soon obtained some interest from Cambridge University Press. The editor who engaged with me was generous in his appraisal of my offering and, in due course, they offered to publish, as a hardback. Of course I was highly delighted and, although I could never consider myself an academic, my editor told me, as I signed my agreement, that, in general, academics were not so much interested in royalties as in being published by Cambridge.

At about that time I served as a representative on the Church of England Evangelical Council, chaired by Dr John Stott and by Bishop Timothy Dudley-Smith and as there happened to be a meeting of Council when my book was published, I ventured to take a couple of copies to show my fellow members something which I felt sure would please them. I am sorry to say there was no enthusiasm. A subsequent review made me realize that there was an undercurrent of feeling, wondering how this non-cleric had managed to do what he was then showing them. And I well remember that, about a year later, a well known and highly respectable central Anglican quarterly asked a very distinguished Evangelical to review my book, but the result was so destructive that they refused to publish. Is it not true that envy afflicts us all, one way or another, and most of us become victims of it at some stage in our careers?

Satisfaction always came to me during my chairmanship at Luckley–Oakfield School in Wokingham, seeing
the school increase its share of the market, maintaining a
strongly Christian ethos and continuously developing its
facilities. I was able to persuade one or two of my friends
to join the governing body and thus enhance its effective-
ness, notable among them being Dick Knight, whom I
knew in my boyhood when we were both Crusaders. He
obtained a double first at Cambridge, got a half blue for
Rugby Fives, and went on, post-war, to head up a house
at Marlborough, at the same time captaining Wiltshire at
cricket. In due course he was appointed headmaster of
Oundle and then of Monkton Combe. During the latter
headship, he had no difficulty in persuading me to go
down to Bath and give a talk to his sixth form on life in
the City. At Luckley–Oakfield, with his great knowledge
of school life, he introduced a brilliant new expertise onto
the board and was very greatly appreciated. Two other
valuable additions to the board which I was able to
achieve were both in the financial field; David Rivett, a
chartered accountant who had, at one time, been engaged
on an internal audit with Coca Cola and Gill Morgan, an
Inspector of Taxes.

Another type of satisfaction came my way at the school
when I took part in an interview, followed by lunch, with
representatives of the Association of Governing Bodies of
Girls Public Schools and the school was duly elected. It is
almost a truism but, in my view worth mentioning, that
the success of any school, in ultimate terms must depend
on a harmonious working relationship between the chair
and the head of the school.

Another memorable occasion at the school came when
Lady Coggan, wife of the then Archbishop of Canterbury,

came to open a new teaching block and I was joined in the ceremony by Lord Caldecote who had always been most supportive and was, I believe, once chairman of the school.

Ambassadors

Jesus, who came as God's ambassadorial Son,
You know how hard it is for us to represent You;
Either they write us off, like John, for being odd
Or else, like You, for being very sociable.

We want so much to represent You faithfully,
To answer questions and, high honour, to convey
The message that all may be reconciled to God,
So guide us to fulfil our role with joy and love.

Randle Manwaring

Dilemma

There was a man who said that he
Was undenominational;
He smote the sects of this and that,
(Deploring the sensational);

He hated ritual and the ruts
Of churches in the High Street,
So joined himself with others such
In quarters down a by-street.

Their clandestine forgatherings
Were mentioned quite *sub-rosa*,
But people passing by would think,
'They've set themselves a poser,

For all their efforts to set up
A non-sectarian basis,
May force, well, even them, at last
To *name* their new oasis'.

Randle Manwaring

F/T Industrial Ordinary Index

Here are the stuttering hopes and fears -
inflation, strikes, the lack of confidence
computerised and brought to print,
spelt out in seismographic form.

This is the shorthand of our world
of manufacture, sales, export,
the quivering ebb and flow of wealth,
moods of the money-go-round of life.

Without prediction of its course,
giving no clue of separate moves,
it offers an inscrutable design,
a kind of financial palmistry.

Randle Manwaring

Chapter 6

As Time Went By

Reflecting on life's experiences, with its ups and downs at all the different levels, I am conscious of a few underlying, but seemingly minor factors which must have been totally relevant, in home life, working life and recreation, whether in wartime or peacetime and which provided the fabric into which patterns are woven, thus forming the full artistry of a humanity. So I am now trying to identify these often intangible, sometimes mysterious influences of a lifetime and, without wishing to appear over pious or hyper spiritual, I must place in prime position my Christian faith – not meaning this in an academic sense although that aspect, intellectually, is important, but I mean a relationship involving complete trust and devotion to the One whom I feel I know as the Son of God. This, from my earliest days and usually in a developing, expanding way, has governed every decision and, although there have been regrettable behavioural lapses, has fired my personality. The results have been many and varied whether at work, at home, in recreation and within the confines of corporate Christianity but how the Spirit of God relates, as intimately as in experience He

111

does, with the spirit of man, must remain something of a mystery but nonetheless is a felt though mystical union. Being so committed also involves being well earthed in a world torn apart and, to a huge extent, in the twentieth century, devastated by disease, famine, war and poverty. But there is no escape. Materialism as a vice now haunts the prosperous west and what the *New York Times* has called the 'Pleasure of Greed' has laid hold of society in an increasing way. The same paper has written of the 'Mania of materialism' and with the modern emphasis on more profits, bigger salaries, bigger pensions and bigger everything else, one is left wondering 'What's the point?' and 'What next?'

Technology drives us all forward as today's inventions quickly become out-of-date. Meanwhile, the inventiveness of man continues to explore possibilities of more effective warfare and now it seems likely that bombs can be delivered by unmanned aircraft. Absolute military supremacy, once measured in terms of colonies and battleships, may soon turn out to be without actual human involvement. Speed of delivery will be the key to diabolical success. In the midst of all this, the Christian remembers that man by nature is tainted but he awaits complete redemption in an entirely new creation. In the meanwhile Winston Churchill's question comes to mind 'If God wearied of mankind?'.

My own personal expression of the faith has especially come to fruition in my strong affection for the songs of Christian belief, usually referred to as hymns and I have always relished the common denominator between hymnody and poetry exemplified, for example, in the compositions of Isaac Watts and Charles Wesley. As I see it, poems of the spirit are a very special link between the inner man and the invisible God and the name given to them is 'hymn'. The close association between poetry and hymnody was emphasized to me when Michael Saward, the author of a very large number of hymns and, before retirement, a Canon at St Paul's Cathedral, London, in telephoning me on another matter, to my surprise kindly suggested that a two-verse poem of mine, appearing in a collection many years ago and entitled, *Bread and Wine*, might well be put forward as a possible hymn. Further, making the point that there can be a real relationship inwardly between an individual and different kinds of poems, I entitled a recent collection *Songs of the spirit*.

I have been vitally interested in poetry for nearly the whole of my life and can remember reciting to myself, when our home was empty - for example *Hiawatha* by Longfellow and Tennyson's *Charge of the Light Brigade*. In my youth, as many of that age did, I fell in love with Rupert Brooke and, in a different way, with the more lyrical works of Kipling, Masefield and Yeats. But Walter de la Mare became, magically, my inspiration, encompassing as he did, a special mystique, a musicality and a seeming naivety in a remarkable way. Poetry at its best, like faith, seeks to explore the hidden world and comes to a fulfilment in all its great works. Poetry dances its way through all the great pleasures of human experience yet seeks to plumb the depths of our despair. All the great themes of life itself surface somewhere in anthologies and yet the final work on anything has not yet been written but woe betide any poet who dares to write echoing lines on a subject already dealt with by the great poets.

When, as a young man, I embarked on a voyage of poetic discovery I struggled to find themes of my own for, I suppose, I had little to write about and no experiences to bring into making a picture. I remained on the fringes of poetry for many years. However, I persisted, read all I

113

could lay my eyes on and had the good fortune, through an introduction by my father, to meet Walter de la Mare, loosely remaining acquainted with him for many years. Like most of my age group I wrestled with *The Waste Land*, fell back on my love of the Georgians and relished the many collections which, in those days before the Second World War, sympathetic publishers brought out. At the time of writing these words, I reckon I have written about 600 poems, most of which have appeared in slim volumes in a period of fifty plus years and over the past twenty years I have averaged about nine new poems a year. I make bold to say that I always write as a Christian, in other words from that view point, but only a percentage of my poems has a specifically Christian theme. When it comes to using the word inspiration (in a non-theological sense) I must be careful what I write but I most definitely feel that for every poem there must be a real moment of conception. One cannot say without anything particularly in mind 'Now today I will write a poem'. But if the soil is kept fertile, the precious seeds will drop in. A poet's notebook however will, in all probability, contain many uncompleted items where the inspiration and enthusiasm were inadequate. 'Poetry is emotion recollected in tranquillity' (Wordsworth) and the element of tranquillity is essential for giving birth. I had many moments of an emotional nature, one way or another, for example whilst abroad or serving in the RAF in the Second World War but I needed the relative tranquillity of home – at least usually – to bring anything to birth in the form of a poem.

When I look back on my earliest poems it is quite obvious that although I found it difficult to achieve originality I took refuge in a certain amount of mysterious thought. Nevertheless, I think I early on sought after

114

structure and form in poetry and varied this element considerably over the years. When one considers that the editor of a good poetry quarterly journal may receive as many as 5,000 contributions in that time and is able only to choose fifty, it is evident that when a poet has an item accepted for publication in such a magazine, there must be a moment of undisguised rejoicing!

Getting collections into print represents another problem although there is a large number of poetry presses which function in this rarefied atmosphere and it is nearly impossible to find a small firm willing to publish a small volume unless most of the poems on offer have already attained credibility and have appeared in magazines. They are the filter. My experiences in the publishing field have been mixed. Often a small press will require the purchase of a number of copies in advance; reviews, when occurring, do not yield much in the way of sales and books shops are very reluctant to stock copies even of a local author. You fall back on a reluctant family and friends!

The poet – even a minor one – ought to see himself or herself as one in the long dynasty of poets – not as another Wordsworth or Hardy – but as one in a field in which all real practitioners, however minor, are engaged. It is an honourable line and great luminosity is not essential. One generation of poetry takes over from another, schools called this or that, Reformed, the Movement, this Post Modernists or whatever do not, in the end, count for very much but there is a sense that one group takes over – 'And Swinburne took from Shelley's lips the Kiss of poetry' – as one Georgian put it. Furthermore, fashions in poetry are always changing, for example there was, post Tennyson, a long-term revulsion against him (I remember a line – 'the drivel and stink of

Tennyson') and, nearer our time, Rudyard Kipling has been almost written off by the pundits. As an example of the ever changing styles of poetry, I would like to record the fact that in each of the years 1955, 1956, 1960 and 1961 the Poetry Society printed one of my poems in their *Poetry Review* but I think I now know that particular market sufficiently well to realize that I would not stand a chance of being accepted if I submitted my poems there today. You learn wisdom.

Over quite a long period I have given talks on poetry to schools in Sussex, notably to the famous Roedean School and on a broad canvas of primary schools, to younger children. I am not suggesting that poems are always easy to fathom or that they each contain one simple interpretation but I do believe in a childlike wonder, seeking an initially simple understanding. A.E. Housman, in his 1933 *Leslie Stephen Lecture*, advises us that 'Even when poetry has a meaning, as it usually has, it may be inadvisable to draw it out...perfect, understanding will sometimes almost extinguish pleasure'. I often reflect that, when the Son of God was faced with a group of children and some of his adult disciples, He didn't tell the youngsters to become like the grown ups but rather that the disciples, those grown men, should become like children in their understanding. Much poetry that I read in modern magazines appears to be esoteric, even obfuscated in the bargain, ceasing to be really enjoyable. Do some poets, I wonder, just write for each other? Every child is at heart a poet when he likes to sit on his father's knee and jog along rhymically or beat time to a nursery rhyme. T.S. Eliot, whose work revolutionized poetry in the twentieth century, advises us that 'the business of the poet is not to find new emotions, but to use the ordinary ones and in working them up into poetry, to express

116

feelings which are not in emotions at all'.

It is, I think, worth remembering that the earliest appreciation of literature is children who are very inventive in the words which they use to recall noises they encounter. The heroes of childhood always have attractively sounding names; for instance those in their romantic or tragic stories. We lose a great deal when we move far away from the fairylands and into the hard-nosed realities, well disguised as truth of, in the modern world. The poet must, however, face up to harsher matters.

I sometimes look back on my visits to countries overseas and wonder whether the startling freshness of the experiences of necessity brought about a new poem. India, Australia, South Africa and the USA come to mind, but I do not think these countries, with all their new attractiveness, produced immediate poetic results. Usually something poetically happened later, often much later. In subsequent years one can recall an experience of great significance although no poem resulted at the time. Perhaps the days were too crowded.

Without further majoring on this factor, I must mention that among some poets there is a feeling of their need to speak out prophetically against the iniquities, injustices and absolute evils of the age in which they live and I sometimes feel like that. In a sense we feel we must warn unless we are fearful of making an unpopular stand. Also, beauty and truth go together and as Keats declares:

> Beauty is truth, truth beauty, that is all
> Ye know on earth, and all ye need to know.

In an age of humanism and unbelief this will be a most unpopular view and I would hesitate to quote this aphorism, from one of our greatest poets, to a modern

117

audience.

A gentle reminder of the dangers of losing our real wealth in the pursuit of new inventions came through in a poem *To a Poet a thousand years hence* written many years ago by James Elroy Flecker:

> I care not if you bridge the seas,
> Or ride secure the cruel sky,
> But have you wine and music still,
> And statues and a bright eyed love.

(Interestingly enough published in a collection of Flecker's poetry by Martin Secker, who years ago favoured poets).

If a poem is set to music and sung by a choir or an individual it reaches a special dimension of acceptability and possible understanding. One of my early poems, *A Song of Sussex*, achieved this form and was sung by various choirs. Later, the first hymn of mine to be included in a collection was put to music by Professor Noel Tredinnick who conducts the orchestra at All Souls, Langham Place, London, and also the annual *Prom Praise* at the Royal Albert Hall. Two other modern books have carried my two hymns and in both cases the tune brings to life the feelings hopefully generated by the words and without wishing to overdo my personal satisfaction, perhaps I may quote the words of Shelley who wrote that, 'Poetry is the record of the happiest and best moments of the happiest and best minds'.

Whenever one of my poems has appeared in an anthology I have rejoiced in finding my way into a collection of the work of kindred spirits, feeling a special acceptance of my offering at a significantly wide and robust level and I always feel sad when a particular publisher gives up an annual event of an anthology, obviously for good financial reasons. Gone are the days when a small publisher would bring out a new slim volume and therefore achieve some sort of recognition or prestige as being a sponsor of the art of poetry and I recall how I would often visit the bookshop run in St James's Square, London where Martin Secker, the publisher, ran his own outlet. He eventually became Secker and Warburg, now part of Random House and from him I eagerly bought, over seventy years ago, volumes by W. H. Davies, published by Jonathan Cape. Even now I can hear the tinkling of the bell which announced the arrival of another customer at Secker's shop.

In considering the relatively unseen special influences in my life, I would like to bring into the picture, in a very personal, mystical way, my Aunt Helen, my father's unmarried sister. She had little formal education but, introduced to the London Library by her brother, she made her way by diligence, courtesy and grace, becoming responsible for all the female staff. Her particular role in the running of the library was to be in charge of the desk to which members came in returning books and for that she was ideally suited. In the course of time she unconsciously established a strong relationship with John Masefield, the Poet Laureate who, at Christmas, would always send her some of his verses and once an autographed copy of a photograph of himself reading a book, with his cat on his lap. Helen had little interests outside the library where she was always the last of the ladies on the staff to choose her holiday period. Always modest and self-effacing she was greatly appreciated there.

At our home, Helen's financial help was vital for, with three sons and a small income, my father was always struggling, but his sister contributed handsomely to the family budget, sometimes helping to buy our clothes etc. Sharing a kitchen with my mother was extremely difficult and produced much tension which usually resulted in floods of tears by Aunt Helen. She had little idea of dress, her hair style was changelessly ancient and she came in for much unwarranted criticism from my mother, her sister-in-law who, before she married, was in the fashion business. They could not have been more different and clashes were a weekly occurrence. When my brother Dennis was born, my aunt took me away to some friends in Peterborough and she always took an interest, unobtrusively for fear of upsetting my mother, in my well-being, often taking me to a local church with her on a Sunday morning and, when I was a teenager, to a service at St Martin-in-the-Fields in London. She encouraged me considerably in my confirmation. From the Library and, realizing my consuming interest in poetry, she brought me many books, doubtless going through the motion of taking them out in her name which she was, of course, perfectly entitled to do. Once, when my father must have felt he needed to take sides with my mother while a female dispute was in progress, he volunteered the information that his sister owed her position at the library to his introduction, apart from which Helen would have had to go into service. It can well be imagined how pleased I was when Helen retired and, having lived in inferior rented accommodation for much of her working life, was persuaded to buy a flat and I was able to introduce her to one in Sutton, Surrey, owned by the Clerical Medical at a time when property prices were reasonably low. I was thrilled. Helen had about her what Cecil Day-Lewis, another Poet Laureate, described as 'the clover-soft authority of the meek'. She had a fairly long retirement in Sutton, visiting the shops and, on Sundays, the local church. When she became dreadfully ill, she was moved into hospital where, almost immediately, they took exception to her very long hair which she had always kept in an enormous bun and this was all cut off for ease of nursing. I am quite sure that if my aunt had been asked at the time if they could cut her hair she would have told them it was quite impossible and when I went to see her in hospital, seeing the short bobbed hair, I could hardly believe my eyes and turned away in disgust and, on her behalf, distress. I shall never be able to measure the influence my Aunt Helen had on my personality - it was a silent, slightly mysterious and a wholly beneficial factor during those impressionable years.

I come now to another somewhat intangible, influential factor in my life – the game of cricket and bringing that into the picture may cause amazement among my non-sporting friends. However, I do so, not because I was a successful cricketer, for my achievements were minimal, but because I feel such an empathy with the game that I can see how much its ethos and culture has become part of me. Or is that unbelievable? Harold Pinter, the English dramatist was quite emphatic – 'I tend to believe', he wrote, 'that cricket is the greatest thing that God ever created on earth' and in *Tom Brown's Schooldays* we learn that 'cricket is more than a game. It's an institution.' One could be forgiven for thinking that, as the game of rugby football was invented at Rugby School, where Tom Brown was immortalized, that game should have been eulogized, instead!

One of my two Headmasters was interviewed by the school magazine and declared that cricket was by far his favourite game adding, 'it is more than a game, it is a code of ethics'. He was certainly a perfectionist and appropriately one year, opening the batting for the staff against the school, he took guard most carefully, using a bail to mark out his position at the crease but was clean bowled first ball. He departed in silence and with his usual dignity. I always feel that getting out first ball or being given out caught behind when you know you didn't snick the ball, produces a resilience and fortitude in adversity which is character forming. There are, of course, other ways of being dismissed wrongfully!

My first representative cricket was played as a member of the XI at Kings College, Wandsworth Common but I played games with my friends on the common every day in the school holidays and on every evening so long as daylight prevailed. Nowadays, when I see recreation grounds and commons in a deserted state, I imagine that all the missing boys and girls are glued either to a TV screen or a computer. Perhaps that is why obesity threatens them.

After I left school, I played in club cricket, first in south London and then in Surrey, always in a minor team but often opening the bowling. Playing for Sutton was rather frustrating at my level for there was only one pitch on the ground, so we always played away from home and sometimes against rather uninteresting opposition or so it seemed. In one team under an elderly captain with the nickname of 'grandpa' I would bat among the lower order and was sometimes not asked to bowl, so for me the match had little to offer. Playing against Seaford in Sussex I experienced my one and only pub crawl (about five stops on the way home) but managed! The members of the half-day Sutton sides were always good company and usually provided transport and occasionally a fixture had a special attraction, for example against Epsom

College on their delightful ground with excellent facilities. When I arranged a fathers versus boys match on the Sutton ground, post war, for Crusaders, I recall that in running after a ball, near the boundary, someone called to me 'Leave it to me, sir'. I got the message, especially when the groundsman was heard to say of me when I was bowling 'You see that gentleman bowling now, every year his run gets shorter and his right arm gets lower'.

I became a member of the MCC in my fifties, not because I was proficient at the game but because of my great interest in it and have enjoyed, for many years, the privilege of sitting in the Long Room or high up in the pavilion. In my later years, for reasons of age and seniority I had the extra privilege of being granted a nominated, reserved seat for test matches. Over the years, I have proposed or seconded for membership many friends and I recall some amusement that, when I joined Midland Bank, word got around that I was an MCC member, with the result that a number of my colleagues were able to persuade me to nominate them. In the banks, playing football or cricket for other than your employer was unofficially looked upon with a mixture of unbelief and disapproval but MCC membership was, of course, different. Similarly, when it was discovered, lunching with colleagues at the bank, that I was a member of the RAF Club, I was asked by several to propose them for membership and was made to realize that, in the big companies, you do not usually look elsewhere to join anything!

My contacts, although slight, with cricket luminaries, have I feel, been very interesting and, first in time, I remember Billy Griffith, two years my junior at my first school, who played for England post-war. At a school assembly our headmaster asked Billy what accounted for his rosy cheeks and he replied 'I eat an apple every day, sir'. David Sheppard, brilliant batsman, who captained Sussex and England, becoming in due course, also famous as Bishop of Liverpool, once came straight from a match at Hove, in which he was slightly injured, to speak at a parents' evening for a beach mission I was running and, very occasionally, I was able to have a few words with him at matches in Arundel on the Duke of Norfolk's ground. Ted Dexter was on my staff for a while at Heaths, as already mentioned and, more recently, at cricket lunches I have met Hubert Doggart, likewise of Sussex and England. We have spoken briefly about an anthology of cricket verse, *A Breathless Hush* which Hubert has edited with David Tayvern Allen (Methuen, 2004) and in the most handsome volume there are about 260 poems about cricket, including items by our Poets Laureate. The book is a clear indication of the fact, which I am endeavouring to highlight, that cricket captures something special in the inner man of so many of us and inspires much philosophy of life itself.

In my experience there is, at all levels, an elitist camaraderie in the game of cricket and, at the higher levels, unknown to me of course, I detect that those in the know, know those who know the top men! As in most other fields of activity it is the personalities of the players which provide the attractive colourings of the game. It is, for example, an Ian Botham (once a Yeovil Crusader, still holding the record for junior throwing the cricket ball in Crusaders Annual Athletics Meeting), Vivian Richards, Tony Grieg and now Andrew Flintoff, who give us the striking make up of cricket. On the other hand, the way in which county cricket has developed, giving all players a good living, has meant the elimination of the amateurs

124

who lent such a rich mixture to the teams.

As I lived through the earlier era I recall with pleasure how each county had its amateur captain, the Cowdreys in Kent, Arthur Gilligan in Sussex, D.R. Wilcox and J.W.H.T. Douglas (Johnny won't hit to-day) Essex, Percy Fender and D. R. Jardine in Surrey, A. W. Carr in Notts, A.G. Hazlerigg in Leicestershire etc. In those days the Gentlemen, as they were called, occupied separate dressing rooms, came out on the field through separate gates and often displayed special caps when fielding, as did Percy Chapman of Kent in his Harlequin number. Then there are, in the long history of cricket, men who stand out for their absolute excellence, W.G. Grace of Gloucestershire, Jack Hobbs of Surrey, Frank Woolley of Kent, and Ranjitsinhji of Sussex, to name but a few.

Adding to the colour of cricket in the counties we have the Band of Brothers in Kent, the Sussex Martlets, the Hampshire Hogs, the Devon Dumplings etc., all reckoned to be leading non-professional sides.

County grounds have their own special charm and some have outstandingly attractive or memorable features, for example, Worcester, Arundel and Taunton. When the table is trimmed and the outfield is neatly cut and stumps are pitched ready for play, the scene is set for glorious friendly combat in summer.

I have gained several delightful friends in watching Sussex at Hove, Horsham and Arundel. Time was when I could include Eastbourne in August but sadly, for commercial reasons I believe, fixtures there are no more. I first saw Sussex play when my family came on holiday to Rottingdean and I also have the happiest memories of playing for that idyllic village when I was a sixteen year old. I was allowed to bowl on most occasions and remember being taken in the team to fixtures at Bramber and Beeding where at one or other place the village blacksmith hit some huge boundaries and sixes, having been up half the night fighting a hayrick fire. In the Rottingdean team were one or two Sussex Martlets (their centenary was in 2005) including one very distinguished gentleman called H.M.O'M. Holman. I often wonder what happened to him.

I am told I am now the oldest player member of Rottingdean, a village close to my heart since Rudyard Kipling lived there. He only moved to Bateman's Burwash, in 1906, I believe for the reason that Rottingdean was becoming too crowded. My parents had booked us into the boarding house run by the cricket club secretary, C.F. Connatty, very close to the cricket ground, so it was easy to become involved there. One year on holiday in that very pleasant village I had the courage to appear in a processional float posing as J.B. Hobbs, complete with bat! Such was my devotion to the game – and my nerve in impersonation!

Among the very attractive county grounds should be mentioned Tunbridge Wells and, when the rhododendrons are in full bloom in early June, a glorious setting is assured. I once had the unexpected experience there of having lunch with the Band of Brothers, in their private tent, one of many always created for the Tunbridge Wells festival. It happened that I was seeking a sit-down luncheon which I always prefer and, encountering the county secretary, he apologized that there were no such facilities but kindly introduced me to the Brothers who took me under their wing.

I have experienced similar hospitality at the Nottinghamshire County Ground when committee members showed kindness and, on the Somerset ground at Taunton, where my old friend Lord Dean (Paul as I first remember him before Margaret Thatcher ennobled him) generously entertained us to lunch. Not unnaturally, he is a vice president of the County Club.

I have not, as yet, been to many of the northern county grounds but I did go to Headingley, Leeds on one occasion and enjoyed meeting Richard Hutton, son of Sir Leonard Hutton, who played for Yorkshire. I was introduced by Patrick Burke, who played in League cricket in the county and was manager in that area for Midland Bank Insurance Services. My duties as his chief insisted that I visited him – at cricket!

One must not underestimate the achievements of those who get into a county second eleven or else make it in one of the minor counties. In the latter I recall playing for an RAF team against a Norfolk eleven and captaining their team was a Mr Falcon who at the time was a director of the Norwich Union. Of those who made county teams at second XI level, I played with Geoffrey Adlard (Middlesex) and Arthur Jones (Surrey), both of whom played, pre-war, for the Clerical Medical in their annual fixture with the Employers Liability at which I opened the bowling. Post-war there was Colin Tait, with me at St James's Square, who kept wicket for Essex II.

From time to time my friend and former Heath's colleague, Derek Newton, has invited me to join him on a Surrey ground, mainly at the Oval where I have been introduced to the Bedser brothers and many members of visiting committees. On one occasion I went to their Guildford ground with Derek and, fortunately for me, we were joined by Graham Gooch and Ted Dexter in a most entertaining conversation. I think that one of the more unusual matches I attended must be the Diocesan Cup Final held in this instance in North London and to this I was taken by Wallace Benn, Bishop of Lewes, the match being between Chichester and Oxford dioceses. The Bishop of Oxford was there supporting his clergy whose star was Andrew Wingfield-Digby, notable for his work in *Christians in Sport* and now vicar of St Andrews, Oxford. Oxford won.

I do not think Country House Cricket, as such, any longer exists, but I once took part in a match of considerable attraction – at Crondall in Hampshire, the home of Lord Anson, a Clerical Medical director. The game was between teams put into the field by the Clerical Medical and the Society's solicitors, Frere, Chelmeley and Nicholson (I hope I had got the right names). We went down from London by coach and were told that to be appointed to the ground staff of Lord Anson you had either to be a retired professional cricketer or once bandsman. I think the weather turned against a game after we arrived and the day developed, apart from lunch, into a charade or two in the marquee.

As I reflect on the various influential unobtrusive factors of a long life, I am aware that there has been a most pleasant and invisible blend between the faith of a Christian, the work of a minor poet and involvement in the world of cricket but not forgetting my Aunt Helen, and I am glad to note that there has never been the slightest conflict between any of them. It was said of Rupert Brooke that, as a boy at Rugby School, he could be seen on the playing fields with a book of poems in one pocket and a cricket ball in the other and for my part I have always found the game of cricket, not just a code of Christian ethics but also suitably harmonious with the fields and pitches, also with melodies of bat and ball and, as I peer into the future, I recall the famous lines of T.S. Eliot in his *Four Quartets*.

Time present and time past
Are both perhaps present in time future,
And time future contained in time past

Coming back to the beginning of my foundations (as I might call them), I recall the words of Robert Browning that:

God is the perfect poet,
Who in his person acts his own creations

And I can see the interlocking, cross fertilizing nature of much of those precious things, I have endeavoured to portray. If I may have succeeded in doing something of that I shall feel satisfied with my testimony to life itself.

Someone wrote (I just forget the source) that the 'Poet, the Soldier and the Priest are the eternal triumphers of earth' and my sense of minor achievement amounts to the fact that I seem to have moved in all three spheres but only in minor, but very related ways.

I cannot allow this chapter to come to an end without endeavouring to clean up what I see to be two common misunderstandings. One is that you might get the impression that there are no Christian poets. In answer, I would emphasize the fact that there have always been Christian poets, that is those who are committed to the faith and who have achieved front-line positions as poets; for example George Herbert and Isaac Watts, their offerings being used as hymns either later, as in the case of Herbert or immediately, as with Watts. They both appear in anthologies of English Poetry. One of my very closest and most valued friends, John Pearce, has assured me that I am a Christian poet and I certainly have no greater ambition than to be known as one, however low in the reckoning I may be placed. My gift in the area of poetry, is something I offer back to my Creator.

The other misapprehension I would like to endeavour to deal with and I think this is one put abroad by the enemy of souls, to give them an opt-out of considering the claims of the Christian faith and that is that Christians are deadly dull, unattractive, unintelligent wimpish people. Now, of course, I realize that there are some Christians in that broad category for our Lord declared that it would be those who felt their need of outside help (a primary requirement) who would be more than likely to receive His gifts but I am glad to say that in my long experience I have had the greatest possible pleasure in meeting thoroughgoing Christians at all levels of society, in all walks of life, in the different occupations, in sporting and literary circles, in the House of Commons and the House of Lords etc. etc. It was the Countess of Huntingdon (1707–91), founder of the body of Calvinistic Methodists known as the Countess of Huntingdon's Connexion, who declared her thanks for the letter 'm' in the verse 'not many wise men after the flesh, not many mighty, not many noble are called'. (St Paul writing to the young Church at Corinth). The Countess was thankful that the New Testament did not say not any ... She, originally greatly helped by the Methodist Revival under Wesley, later felt the need to attract into the Church some of the upper classes, so formed a group of chapels (what a reversal of subsequent vague class divisions!)

So I rest my case. I give thanks to my Creator for the part He has given me in His plans – the mix of life, which I have found so satisfying.

Children of the Regiment

A few years ago, as girls they watched
furtively, half-interested, reading a book
then, with marriage to a county hero,
each settled for being a cricketing wife.

Now, with their babies, they continue watching
at home matches, engrossed in the welfare
of the little ones but when their men come home
from away fixtures just deal with dirty washing.

Once, their grandmothers, sent back to England
for their education, were children of another regiment,
the males serving at Simla or Snooty Ooty
and playing polo for the Bengal Lancers.

Wives of the county team, they enjoy a fame
for a few swift summers while husbands keep
a place in the premier side, with children
of once competing women and competitive males.

Randle Manwaring

Cricket Final

Gloucestershire and Somerset,
finalists at Lords,
join in friendly joust,
knocking down the stumpy.

From Cotswolds and Blackdown Hills,
from Quantocks and the Mendips,
from Forest of Dean and Bristol,
they came with ale and scrumpy.

Botham, Garner and Richards,
plus Grace, Graveney and Procter,
watching, made each others' rides
very distinctly bumpy.

Randle Manwaring

The Club Man

Every club needs one but only one.
He is the answer to every whim;
helps at the bar, stacks the chairs,
shouts to a player, steady Jack
and calls his fellow members lads.

He moves around at quite a pace
and even in the hottest weather
sports the club tie; the embodiment
of social life, chain-smoking and
beer-bellied, clubbable, alone.

Randle Manwaring

Index

Huxley, Thomas, 6